C000101446

Twelve Ancient Doorways
to
Freedom

Twelve
Ancient Doorways
to
Freedom

Discovering Twelve Unseen Supernatural Doorways
From Life's Adversities to Favor and Wellbeing

Choose this day life or death, blessing or curse.
Deuteronomy 30:19

Otto Bixler

Copyright 2022

Twelve Ancient Doorways to Freedom

Published July 2022

Copyright ©2021 Otto C. Bixler Jr

The right of Otto C. Bixler Jr to be identified as the author of this work has been asserted by him in accordance with the Copyright Designs and Patent Act 1988.

All rights reserved. No part of this publication may be reproduced or transmitted in any form or by any means, electronic or mechanical, including photocopy, recording or any information storage and retrieval system, without permission in writing from the publisher.

Unless otherwise indicated, biblical quotations are taken from the New American Standard Bible®, Copyright © 1960, 1963, 1968,1971, 1972, 1973,1975, 1977, 1995 by The Lockman Foundation. Used by permission. (www.Lockman.org)

Extracts marked NIV are taken from the Holy Bible, NEW INTERNATIONAL VERSION®. Copyright © 1973, 1978, 1984 by Biblica, Inc. All rights reserved worldwide. Used by permission.

NEW INTERNATIONAL VERSION® AND NIV® are registered trademarks of Biblica, Inc. Use of either trademark for the offering of goods or services requires the prior written consent of Biblica US, Inc.

British Library Cataloguing-in-Publishing Data
A catalogue record for this book is available from the British Library.

Extracts marked Amp are taken from the Holy Bible, The Amplified Bible, 1965, by Zondervan Publishing House Copyright © 1962 Zondervan, Amplified Old Testament

ISBN 979-888525417-5

Cover design by Linda Nichols

Acknowledgments

The first acknowledgment is to God Himself who has taken us from the wrong side of many of the spiritual doorways mentioned in this book, given us insight and understanding, orchestrated many personal adventures across the nations to help others pass through the twelve doorways to a better life, and now in enabling the writing of this book so that others whom we will never meet may receive freedom from the many unsuspected causes of difficulties in their lives.

Secondly, I wish to acknowledge all of those who so kindly listened to me and encouraged me to write *Twelve Ancient Doorways to Freedom.* Finally, but not last on the list in my heart, are those who came alongside me in editing, preparing this work and pre-reading the various drafts for the relief of the many who have yet to pass through God's ancient doorways to personal freedom. The primary editors, in the order of their processing of the text, are Lynne Vick, Barbara Naylor, and Roger Bullard. The cover artwork is by Linda Nichols.

Contents

Twelve Ancient Doorways to Freedom

Prologue

Twelve ancient doorways to a better life and the keys to open them are revealed in the chapters of this book. They are doors hidden in the ancient texts of the Bible that we have clearly identified and explained to make it easy for your passage. On one side of each door lies a surprising cause of pain and adversity in our lives. On the other side lies the pathway to God's favor and blessings.

> *Then I will give [you] ... [in] the valley of Achor (pain) a door[way] of hope.*
>
> *Hosea 2:15*

My wife Sharon and I have brought many men, women, and children through these passageways to unexpected relief, well-being and sometimes prosperity. Hear their stories of how they escaped from adversity and read the hidden-in-plain-sight principles that were applied to obtain their rewards. You will learn whether you, perhaps unsuspectingly, are on the wrong side of some of these doors and how to walk through should you need to do so. Each chapter explains clearly how to unlock a passageway to personal favor.

If you find yourself needing to pass through any of these doorways and you take the steps prescribed, your life will be transformed. Most chapters include at least one amazing, illustrative real-life story taken from nearly forty years of public and private ministry. These stories will help you understand and use the doorways to freedom and blessings.

Together the stories, biblical truths, and insights gained from decades of experience form a richly woven carpet of understanding. Should one dare ask God for a ride, the sincere might climb aboard this carpet to be carried, Aladdin-like, on your own adventures, soaring with Him into more discoveries and helping others to achieve the same blessings you received as you passed through the hidden doorways of God. We know it works; that's what happened to us!

Introduction

Miracles, Ancient Doors and Keys
Your Travel from the Lands of Disfavor to Favor in the
Natural and Supernatural Realms

On the cover of this book and in the Prologue, promises were made for your life, promises that can be received. They are rewards for a journey taken, your journey. For most people embarking on this passage, there is a new opening of the eyes required, a paradigm shift. Of course, you can just jump into the chapters of the journey; but to maximize your rewards, there is a bit of preparation needed for you have never been this way before. Please read on. We want you to receive everything offered.

We have much to share with you: discoveries of truth, miracles, ancient doors, and the promise of rewards. Few find these doorways, and fewer still know how to pass through to get their blessings. Let's take those first steps toward your blessings now, your steps of preparation.

First, we're going to be exploring miracles on your journey toward blessings, something many have never seen or believed can happen. Then we will be giving you the keys to unlock your personal miracles and blessings. But first, let's learn about miracles, miracles that happen today.

Miracles

Sometimes miracles just happen. In a sudden, surprise squall of God's love, blessings shower down from heaven, drenching us in His mercy and kindness.

At other times we're instantly deputized to step in, catalyze, be caught up in, and facilitate bringing God's blessing to someone else.

Real-life Story

It was the evening of Robbie Caskwright's first death. We were seated in the last row by the door of the packed-out Christian meeting. Earlier he passed us as he made his way out. It must have been twenty minutes or so before Angela, a registered nurse, poked her head around the door and whispered, "Otto, Sharon, come quickly. It's Robbie!" We were jerked suddenly from absorbing heavenly truths into the cold reality of earthly life.

As we followed Angela out into the foyer, there was Robbie, awkwardly sprawled on the leather reception area couch, dead.

Tersely she recounted in her best, authoritative but subordinate nurse'ese, as if we were the doctors, "He came out here, sat down and died. I've tried mouth-to-mouth resuscitation and heart massage, and I can't get him back. I've called the paramedics."

Somehow, we were instantly deputized and thrust into the drama. It seemed best to lay Robbie on the floor. At that moment, his widow rounded the corner. In one glance she took in the scene and knew Robbie was dead! The moments blurred into one as she threw herself onto his dead body, wailing a death lament. Amidst the tragedy, the Lord spoke into my heart: "This is not Robbie's time." It seemed like time itself was frozen, but I was free to move as I saw and heard myself speak words that were not mine: "Death, let go of Robbie!" Then I called Robbie to come back out of the heavenly realms into his body, and I asked God to reattach the silver cord to hold his soul and spirit in place once again.

Robbie's eyes fluttered open and he sat up alive, not to die again for another twenty years after a long, rich, fulfilled and completed life. The paramedics and the hospital staff confirmed that Robbie had suffered a fatal heart attack. His resurrection was a miracle.

Things like this have happened to Sharon and me before and indeed they are miracles.

Real-Life Story

Martha, the church secretary, was escorting us to our car. It had been a God-blessed women's meeting that afternoon in her church. As we were stepping out into the late afternoon sunlight, God spoke to me: "I want you to pray for her." I knew what He wanted. Martha was a lifelong hunchback with a large protrusion at her right shoulder, something I had never had to deal with before.

Eagerly she replied, "Yes," when I asked if she would like me to pray for her. I didn't really know what to do, but I decided to speak something in the Lord's name and lay my hand on the deformity. As I touched the afflicted area, all I could get out of my mouth was, "In Jesus' name," and the hump collapsed like a child's toy balloon being released of air.

It was a miracle.

Supernatural Sourcing of Miracles

Today most consider that germs, bacteria, microbes and viruses can bring sickness, infirmity, illness and death into a person's life. But that belief would not have been so prevalent before Leeuwenhoek perfected the microscope in the late 17th century, allowing us to see things that were not discernible to the unaided eye. Today we can accept electricity, atomic radiation, and magnetism as demonstrable science. But somehow, when we get to spiritual matters, the pragmatist in us seems to spring to life, both in Christians and non-Christians alike.

We would not be writing this book except that unbelief abounds worldwide when it comes to spiritual cause and effect. The concept of miraculous and spiritual causes for earthly conditions and events seems to be abhorrent to most, probably because we have had no previous, personal involvement with such things. But this very unbelief keeps us from experiencing the relief God has provided for many of our life's problems.

Many believe that there was an actual Jesus who died on the cross for our sins so we might enter heaven (although we've never seen that place). Few—even Christians—have a grasp that Jesus also paid for our sins on the cross to give us well-being for our earthly life. But He did so. Each year some six million people go to Lourdes, France, hoping they might be miraculously helped or healed. Others wear copper bands, magnets, amulets and medals, ingest powdered rhino horns and other materials, or seek help from various rituals, ceremonies and deities. But most never find relief through these ineffective activities.

Yet miracles do happen, and we believe in them. And that is because we have seen miraculous healing and rescues. At some point in our lives, most of us wish for a miracle, some kind of favor that defies reason in its accomplishment. In ancient Greek drama, a point was often reached when the hero/ heroine would be caught facing certain death with no possible extraction from the situation. "Will this end in tragedy?" the audience is wondering. Then comes miraculous deliverance—the term is *deus-ex-machina*. A "god" is lowered via a crane into the drama to redeem the situation without recompense, process or explanation.

Real-Life Story

We were ministering in a small church near Nyíregyháza, Hungary, when a mother came up to me and revealed that her seven-year-old daughter was blind in one eye. I had a great conviction of spirit that God wanted to heal the girl, but God asked me to have her schoolmates pray for her, laying their hands over the blind eye. As the children asked God (for a miracle) to heal the eye, immediately she began to have sight where there was none before. The pastor of the church covered the girl's formerly only good eye and led her around the church, having her read various wall hanging texts, which she did flawlessly.

It was a bona fide miracle.

In the real-life stories just recounted, one common thread linking them together is that each miracle was initiated unilaterally by God (even if we were used by God to accomplish them); it was not man seeking help and prayers being answered. A question we might ask then is, "What about man-initiated miracles?"

Is it possible to ask for God's mercy and see Him bring that requested help? Is there any circumstance in which we can initiate a miracle that will help people? By now you may be expecting the answer is "Yes," but how can it be? We'll be examining the "how's" throughout this book.

By definition, a miracle is an event not explicable by natural or scientific laws. Often these events are attributed to a supernatural being (outside the laws of nature), i.e., a god, a magician, a miracle worker, a now dead saint (like Mary, Peter, Christopher), or some kind of religious leader or guru. Usually, miracles are associated with a beneficial action towards a person or group of people. And miracles often seem to come not from any merited favor nor compensation paid nor at a particular time. Some who visit Lourdes, France, or other "holy" pilgrimage sites may make vows to God or make financial offerings to attain favor or healing, but others do not. In the end, most go home from these places without the favor they were seeking.

But another kind of miracle exists, one not explainable by natural or scientific laws. It is a miracle attainable by any Christian, one which can happen without the favor of a dead saint, religious leader, guru, idol, magician, special food, substance, ritual or incantation. It can be obtained in any country using any language and is not conditional on being particularly religious. It is this type of miracle we focus on in this book. You will discover how to initiate miracles, give blessings to others and receive miracles for yourself. Often the need for a miracle comes from being in a bad place in our life and our release can be related to how we got there.

Blessings and Curses

When we wish for a miracle for ourselves, it's usually because we're in dire straits in or under the threat of disfavor. In Biblical terms, we may be under a curse. The miracle itself is what moves us through the doorway from the land of curse (pain, disfavor or adversity) into the land of blessing (favor, health, prosperity and well-being). But to obtain this miracle, first we must examine the reasons for our dwelling in disfavor.

God has given us a roadmap, an instruction manual if you will, to let us know what behavior will result in favor and what will result in adversity. This instruction manual is called the Bible. God has made it possible for us to improve our lot in life by understanding and applying certain principles (provisions of God) that are documented in the Bible. However, these principles are seldom known, understood, or used by most Christians.

Within the pages of this book, we are illuminating these principles for you so that you can pick them up and use them to help yourself, your family and others. In a sense, these provisions are doorways to supernatural benefits. As you discover the available doorways, you will be able to use God's keys to freedom to initiate passage to the land of blessings. (We'll get to the keys later in this *Introduction*.)

Passage through doorways between the land of blessings and the land of adversity is accessible to us through understanding basic spiritual laws. Many of these doorways are based on the first five books of the Bible (the Pentateuch). Some are clearly stated in Deuteronomy 27, where Moses recites a long list of curses—adversity that exists on the wrong side of these doorways. As you read through the chapters in this book, you will begin to see many other Scriptures in God's "instruction book" to help you obtain your own personal miracles, taking you from adversity to blessing.

So far, we've been a little abstract, so let's frame in the spiritual discussion with something practical, and then we'll compare the practical with the spiritual realm.

Natural Lands of Disfavor

Favor and disfavor might be a gentler way of exploring this topic. Let's bridge into this first by looking at the natural realm and then exploring the spiritual realm and its principles. First here's a simple natural example.

If our family were farmers and they had emigrated to a land where there was sparse rainfall and depleted soil, then they would have experienced small harvests, poor crops and a difficult life. Several generations later, when we are born into a situation that was not of our making, we are in an unfavorable place because of our family's past generational decisions. But by now the family has developed coping mechanisms, adopted the culture and language of the region, and has a rich resource in familial relationships; yet they suffer because of a poor or uninformed choice by their forbearers.

Spiritual Lands of Disfavor

Spiritually, many of us are in such a situation resulting from the uninformed choices we or our generational lineage made. While it is quite clear in the natural case of farmers living in a poor climate with a poor soil condition where we are held in the prison of cultural attachment and acclimation, it is not so obvious in the spiritual realm. This is what we will explore further to bring you relief by taking you through the *twelve ancient doorways* to freedom that God has made available—in a sense these are miracles available through application of God's statutory provisions. Let's explore this further to see how it works. You don't have to be a theologian to discover and use these doorways of escape from adversity.

Our behavior takes us to spiritual places that are not rich in soil nor favorable in climate to where either we or our family before us have emigrated. We have arrived in these spiritual places of disfavor by uninformedly or otherwise not following God's ways. The Bible calls this divergence from God's ways sin. We have been speaking of doorways to relief, but often there are locks on doors to keep the unauthorized out. To pass through we will also need keys to unlock the benefits we are seeking.

Spiritual Keys:
Unlocking the Doorways to Favor

As we have explained, God's instruction manual contains keys to receiving the miracles we need for favor in our life.

Below you will find two Scriptures, one from the Old Testament and one from the New Testament, with keys to receiving your miracles (These will work on all twelve of the doors in the following chapters). First the Old Testament Scripture:

> *"If [because* of the people's disobedience*] I shut up the heavens so that there is no rain, or if I command the locust to devour the land, or if I send pestilence among My people, and My people who are called by My name humble themselves and pray and seek My face and turn from their wicked ways, then I will hear from heaven, will forgive their sin and will heal their land. "Now My eyes will be open and My ears attentive to the prayer offered in this place. "*
> *2 Chronicles 7:13-15*

In the New Testament passage from the book of James, we see a similar step-by-step statutory provision of God for relief from adversity.

> *Is anyone among you sick? Then he must call for the elders of the church and they are to pray over him, anointing him with oil in the name of the Lord; and the prayer offered in faith will restore the one who is sick, and the Lord will raise him up, and if he has committed sins, they will be forgiven him. Therefore, confess your sins to one another, and pray for one another so that you may be healed.*
> *James 5:14-16*

Now let's simplify these keys for your personal use. These provisions of God for relief and remedy are outlined below as a step-by-step process.

The First Key — Confession

In both passages, we see the element of confession—we must come before God and before fellow believers in the Lord, humbling ourselves by admitting specifically how we and/or our family have diverged from God's pathways (sinned) by acting in a way that God has told us not to act in the Bible.

The Second Key — Repentance

Intrinsic in confession is an understanding that sin must be stopped or turned away from. Without your decision and the action of turning away from the land of curse (where wrong behavior has taken you), you will not be able to walk through the doorways to the land of blessing. The doorways to the land of blessing may be entered only by those whose hearts have been turned toward obedience to God's ways. Confession of our sinful position (i.e., admitting our guilt) is a necessary step, but it is not enough. We must repent (turn) toward obedience to God's ways.

The Third Key — Forgiveness
(Through the Blood of Jesus)

In this third step, you need to ask God for forgiveness. It also helps to have someone hear your confession. This person can evaluate your repentance and discern the condition of your heart. He or she will then speak forgiveness to you in the name of Jesus and by His precious blood (see John 20:23). As with the other keys, you are engaging in a spiritual transaction only available to those belonging to God.

The Fourth Key—Healing/Restoring (In the Name of Jesus)

To assist with restoration, the person hearing your confession and statement of repentance speaks the restoration process into being; e.g., "I now command this curse (of disfavor) to stop. The sentence of curse is now broken through the shed blood of Jesus. Everything causing this curse (disfavor) must leave in Jesus' name. I now speak healing and restoration to you in the name of Jesus and release you from the curse of this sin."

Becoming Part of God's Family

The keys to the doorways of escape are spiritual in nature. They are intended for those who belong to God, to His family through receiving Jesus as Lord and Savior. For many reading this book, church attendance may be a normal practice, while for others it can be something of a mystery. Whether you attend church or not, it is vitally important for you to have a relationship with God to obtain the freedom offered in this book. Some of us have had bad experiences with those calling themselves Christians, or with church itself. Based on these experiences, you might be a little reluctant to be involved with either. Relax and do not let some bad experiences get in the way of receiving what God has to offer you through the twelve doorways to a better life.

Please go to the Appendix to find out how to become part of God's family and the benefits that He has for you. It is quite simple. Even if you are a church attender, please work your way through the Appendix.

In the next twelve chapters, your eyes will be opened to twelve doorways of escape from adversity. Choosing to go through a doorway using the before-mentioned keys will put you on the pathway to favor, escaping very real troubles that cause disfavor of all kinds and sometimes physical disabilities. Read on to discover some surprising things God wants to rescue you from. If the keys described above seem a little abstract right now, don't despair: As you read each chapter, we will help you see, understand and step-by-step be led to freedom and well-being through the use of them.

Twelve Ancient Doorways to Freedom

Chapter 1

The First Doorway
What Goes Around Comes Around

Entering the Book

We promised you hidden doorways to travel from places of adversity in your life to favor and well-being. However, most of us are unaware that some of life's adversity can be escaped. Our usual reactions are just to adapt to life's conditions, never thinking there might be a cause behind some of our difficulties and, therefore, we never search for a remedy. As the chapters unfold, you will be discovering that there are difficulties having causes that can be removed from your life. Although some of the chapters may not touch your life directly, others will have a powerful effect on you.

A Saying with a Source

How many times have we said or heard others say, "What goes around, comes around"? It represents so much truth that the expression often occurs in day-to-day conversation. Did you know this truth is actually rooted in a Bible Scripture?

The Spiritual Law of Sowing and Reaping

Here's the source of the "What Goes Around, Comes Around" expression:

> *Do not be deceived: God cannot be mocked. A man reaps what he sows.*

> Galatians 6:7 NIV
> (See also Hosea 10:12–13)

1

Now, let's see how this works and how this spiritual mechanism might possibly touch your life.

Real-Life Story

Some years ago, a man, let's call him Johnathan (not his real name), came to us seeking relief from chronic headaches. We prayed a simple prayer for healing, but nothing happened. As we began to question him, we learned that he also experienced frequent head injuries, even around the home. But there seemed to be no point of origin for his condition.

As we asked the Holy Spirit to show us the cause, suddenly Johnathan remembered a family story. Many generations back in a rural farming area, a severely deformed baby was born into his family. Not knowing what to do with this baby, the father took it out to the barn area and, using a piece of wood, killed the child by a blow to the head. The sin was murder.

We led Johnathan through a prayer of repentance for the violent murder carried out by his family and a prayer of forgiveness towards them for opening up this spiritual doorway of punishment into his life. As we then ministered to him, proclaiming freedom through the name and blood of Jesus, Johnathan was instantaneously healed (passed completely through the spiritual doorway of sowing and reaping to freedom). When we saw him again months later, he reported having suffered no more headaches and was no longer receiving head injuries. He was set free from the consequences prescribed by the Law of Sowing and Reaping.

In telling this story, we've introduced another element: the concept of generational sin and its results in the present day. While we cannot be kept out of heaven for the wrongdoing of our forbearers, we can suffer here on earth from the consequences of their ungodly decisions and actions (Lamentations 5:7). We've seen many set free as they repented (used the *Second Key*, the key of repentance in unlocking the doorway to freedom – see *Introduction*) for both their own wrongdoings and those committed by their families who came before them. It is important to know, however, that at the entrance to heaven we will only be held responsible for our own deeds, including all of our personal sins on earth.

> *For we must all appear before the judgment seat of Christ, so that each one may be recompensed for his deeds in the body, according to what he has done, whether good or bad.*
> 2 Corinthians 5:10

One part of Jesus' work on the cross was to make it possible for us to have eternal life, but the other part was to make it possible for us to be healed and set free from the consequences of sin in this life (James 5:15-16). We've prayed with many over the years who have been set free from present-day problems as they have repented of their (and/or their family's) sins of the past.

Mirroring of Our Misdeeds
In our real-life story above, we see a mirroring of the blow to the newborn child's head in Jonathan's continued suffering with head afflictions. In another story, this one

recounted in the book of Judges, we see a similar mirroring, this time in the life of a wicked king.

> *Judah went up, and the LORD gave the Canaanites and the Perizzites into their hands, and they defeated ten thousand men at Bezek. They found Adoni-bezek [the king] in Bezek and fought against him, and they defeated the Canaanites and the Perizzites. But Adoni-bezek fled; and they pursued him and caught him and cut off his thumbs and big toes. Adoni-bezek said, "Seventy kings with their thumbs and their big toes cut off used to gather up scraps under my table; as I have done, so God has repaid me."*
>
> *Judges 1:4–7*

In this case, the king was aware of his wrongdoing and immediately understood what had happened to him. But many of us are suffering with symptoms or consequences of transgressing God's ways, and we have not recognized the source of our problems. When God shows us our wrongdoing, why we are suffering, it is frequently as obvious to us as it was to this pagan king. In most cases, when God has made evident the source of our suffering, we may agree with Him, confessing the sin, repenting, and receiving forgiveness in the name of Jesus. This process begins to release us from the consequences prescribed by God's law for that particular wrongdoing.

Before we go any further, we need to clarify our use of the word *sin*. While both Christians and non-Christians are familiar with this word, let's just sharpen up our understanding here as it is pivotal in our understanding of each of the hidden doorways we are examining. In its most

4

simple definition, *sin* just means "we have transgressed a behavioral or thought/attitude boundary set by God."

In this chapter's first story, the departure from God's ways was the sin of murder, something most would understand. In the second story, the sin is the maiming and suffering of the seventy kings, brought on by the wicked king, Adonibezek. In this chapter we are not highlighting a particular transgression, but rather a doorway by which earthly suffering may come supernaturally into our life. Understanding the principle helps us discover the sources of trouble in our life, the doorway through which they came, and therefore the way of escape.

Weeds, Corn or Watermelon

If we plant weeds (disobedience), how could we expect to reap corn or watermelons (blessings/favor)? Yet, many of us are surprised when trouble comes our way and we have forgotten or never realized that an earlier action on our or our family's part is responsible. The timing between our action and the judgment of God is often great enough that we miss making the connection and we continue to suffer, not realizing a doorway to relief and freedom exists.

The Law of Sowing and Reaping is similar to the Law of Judgment (highlighted in the next chapter) in that the temporal sentence we receive—punishment or disfavor— will often have a similarity to our transgression. The difference between this law and the Law Judgment examined in Chapter 2 is that sowing and reaping is not specifically linked to judging others, but it could be. It is a general legal principle that helps us understand what "comes around" is very similar to "what goes around."

5

Simply put, the seed (sin) that you plant will often result in a growth that looks similar to the seed (original deed) of disobedience. And as a single seed can reap a harvest, sowing good or bad can reap even more than the original action.

Interestingly, our present suffering may be the result of sins we committed either before or after receiving Jesus as our Savior. There is no difference in the consequences of sin, whether its origin was before or after our salvation. It is surprising to many that our salvation, while it assures our entrance to heaven, does not prevent our suffering for prior sins while we're here on earth. Further, these same sins, if not confessed and repented for here on earth, will have to be accounted for at the doorway to heaven and will cost us something (see 2 Corinthians 5:10 above and 1 Timothy 4:8).

In the first three chapters of this book, we are examining how spiritual laws, The Law of Sowing and Reaping, the Law of Judgment, and the Law of Forgiveness affect our destiny, and how the benefits we can enjoy here on earth are related to our thinking about and actions towards God and others. Taken together, these spiritual laws show us how important it is that we forgive others, not holding their faults against them; we will either receive goodness or difficulty in our lives depending upon how well we do in our hearts and actions. It's very simple. Much of what we receive or experience in our lives can be influenced by what we think, say, and do. Jesus gave us a summary in the "Golden Rule":

In everything, therefore, treat people the same way you want them to treat you, for this is the Law and the Prophets.

Matthew 7: 12

King David, with his insight to God's ways, sheds some light on the *Law of Sowing and Reaping* in Psalm 18:

The LORD has rewarded me according to my righteousness,
*   according to the cleanness of my hands in his sight.*
To the faithful you show yourself faithful,
*   to the blameless you show yourself blameless,*
to the pure you show yourself pure,
*   but to the devious you show yourself shrewd.*

Psalm 18: 24-26 NIV

In summary, the Law of Sowing and Reaping may be explained as: If we do good in our life here on earth, good comes back to us; and if evil, then evil comes back to us; but for both it always returns in multiplied form, just as seed when planted multiplies itself. Now with our new understanding of this powerful but simple law, we need to ask ourselves and God, "What have I sown against God's ways that is now producing bad fruit in my life?" You might need to take a little time with the Lord to discover some of these personal areas of transgression. Please remember that your family, nation, or a group to which you may have belong(ed) could have sin patterns in its history that now affect you because of your association.

The best practice in prayers of release is to have a "Prayer Partner" stand with you for this process; i.e., have at least one other Christian witness your repentance and speak

7

forgiveness, healing and release to you in the name of Jesus. Of course, you can pray through the issues in this chapter on your own, just you and God, but we have provided scripted prayers for both you and a prayer partner to facilitate your passage from disfavor in life to favor.

For those sin sources brought to light, you can then confess them, repent, and receive forgiveness. These prayers of release will effectively stop the ongoing development of new trouble from this source.

You must realize, though, that the Law of Sowing and Reaping functions to multiply whatever you do. If you were blessing others, then more blessings will return to you. If you were troubling others by your behavior, then you will receive more trouble than you troubled others with. Just like planting seed, you will get a crop of whatever you plant. And even though you stop sinning (sowing trouble), your old crop of trouble may continue to come up in your life even after you stop (repent). You may not see immediate relief, but eventually you will be better off.

What Goes Around, Comes Around
Stepping Through the Doorway of Release

Use the following prayer for each of the Sowing and Reaping areas you have discovered. You are now at the doorway of escape. Just a little more work for freedom. Get ready for relief and blessings.

Your Prayer and Declarations

Dear Heavenly Father, I come to You now in the name of Jesus. Lord, I confess that I (and/or my family) have sinned by (tell God here what was done wrong—

8

where, when, with whom or to whom, etc.). Lord, I am
sorry that I/we did this because it is against You and
Your ways. I choose to turn from this sin and not to do
this again. I choose by an act of my free will to forgive
myself and/or my family members who came before
me and opened this doorway to the land of curse.
Please help me, Holy Spirit, to walk away from
practicing this sin in my life. Heavenly Father, please
forgive me in the name of Jesus and through His
precious blood. Amen.

Prayer Partner Speaks*

In the name of Jesus, I speak forgiveness to (your
name) for the sin of (name the sin that you just
confessed). I also claim the blood of Christ between
(your name) and the (name the sin practiced by his/her
family). In the name of Jesus, I command every spirit
from the practice of this sin to leave (name of the
brother/sister) now. [Wait a moment for God to do
this.]
Repeat this last command for each sin renounced.
Check with the Holy Spirit to be sure that any
deliverance that was necessary has taken place.]

*Please note that the Holy Spirit may bring up issues in this process that
He wants to have uncovered—things that were, perhaps, not known.
Listen and do what He says. Further, when commanding any spirits of
curse to leave, watch to see what God is doing and give Him some time
to bring about the cleansing and release. If possible, a process of
restoration with the estranged parent/parents should be considered.

Chapter 2

The Second Doorway
I Would Have Done It Better

The Pleasure of Judgment

Judging others comes easily to us. It happens so fast in our hearts that we scarcely realize what we're doing. First, we observe someone's performance in a situation; then we measure them against our own self-image, often deciding, "I would have done it better." Unconsciously, we have pushed ourselves up and the other person downward. (Somehow there often is a pleasure in feeling superior to others.) In its actions, judgment can be similar to unforgiveness, which we will examine in Chapter 3. Like unforgiveness, it has dire consequences in our earthly life. It also leads to loss of heavenly blessings after death. Let's further explore what judging is so as to discover how we might be entangled in it. Once we understand judgment and its unpleasant consequences, we will be able to leave the land of trouble into which we may have unknowingly entered through this hidden doorway.

Real-Life Story

Let's examine how judgment works in a person's life. This story is one that I'll never forget as it is from my own life. The problem we have in recognizing cause and effect in our transgressions is that often our disobedience happened many years in the past; perhaps it occurred even in our childhood and has been long forgotten. So it was in this case.

We had not been married very long when I noticed an unwelcome change in my wife's behavior: she was becoming increasingly late when getting ready to go somewhere with me. Before we married, I remembered that she was as precise as a Swiss watch in her appointments. But now it seemed that she could not be on time no matter where we were going.

As a recently born-again Christian with only a few years' experience in godly communication and living, I was struggling with how to communicate my displeasure to her. At first, I only managed a few gentle reminders about time passing when we needed to be somewhere. But my wife had noticed "her problem" and had already begun to take responsibility for her increasing tardiness. Unknown to me, whenever we were going somewhere together, she systematically began to get ready earlier.

Over a period of time, she began correcting the situation by starting to prepare fifteen minutes earlier, but she was still late. So, she started to get ready a half-hour earlier, but she was still late. As the months rolled by, it seemed that nothing could get her out of the house on time to go somewhere with me.

As time went on, I became more and more intolerant of her lateness. It was really causing our relationship— and me—a problem. Finally, one day I could stand it no longer as I watched her slowly begin to dress, going through her clothes deciding what to wear. It was clear we were going to have another "late experience." I exploded in anger, "Can't you ever be on time? You're just like my moth...e...r!" The last word sort of

12

squeezed its way from my mouth as I attempted to stop it. I was so startled at what I was saying; I instantly recognized it as a judgment from the past now surfacing.

In a split second my face turned crimson with embarrassment, as my sin lay exposed for both of us to see. We knew full well what a "judgment" is and there was instant recognition that afternoon in our bedroom. Our eyes locked on each other. The expression of guilt and shame on my wife's face for being late one more time transformed into the expression of a trial lawyer as he cross-examines a witness in the courtroom. Glaring at me, she stepped closer, hands now on her hips. A slightly superior smile began to form on her lips as she demanded, "Tell me about your mother!"

I instantly knew that I was a "dead man"—tried, convicted, and sentenced, all in the space of a few moments. The "condemned" one was exonerated and her accuser, i.e., me, now stood guilty.

As my sin rose to the surface, I began to see what was at the root of my judgment. You see, a dawning social awareness happens to most teenagers, making them overly sensitive towards embarrassment. This sensitivity manifests when real or imagined differences are perceived between us or our family members and others outside the family. At that age, we desperately want to be the same as everyone else.

So it had been with me. Earlier in my life I had begun to notice that my family was often late to social functions and it embarrassed me. I began to believe that it was my mother's fault for not getting ready quickly enough. We continued to be late as a family, and I started to judge my mother. I can still remember the day that I finally verbalized it as I walked out of the family home to go somewhere when preparations were progressing too slowly for me. I slammed the door behind me, exclaiming, "I don't know about the rest of you, but I'm going now, and I am going to be on time!" The words were dripping with judgment, accusation, and self-righteousness as I stomped out the door.

My sin caused my wife to be late. As she later recounted, "It was like walking through glue each time we tried to go somewhere together. I just could not move faster, and things always happened to delay me."

The transgression of God's commandment not to judge puts the Law of Judgment in motion, and the sentence under this law is often amazing in the way it mirrors the sin itself. It is not that we are going to be excluded from heaven by the sin, but rather that we will suffer here on earth. In this case, judging my mother resulted in suffering through my wife; but it came years later. As we saw in the previous chapter, God is not mocked; what we sow we will reap (see Chapter 1), i.e., our behavior has consequences. Our difficulty is that we often don't recognize current suffering as a result of past sin because it may occur years after the sin.

As I confessed and repented of my sin of judgment that afternoon, God set my wife free of being the just implement of my punishment. She is no longer chronically late. Now, more often, I am the late one!

Judgment Often Works Out in Family

The negative rewards for our sin of judgment are not always carried out through our spouses, but when they are, it is often as a result of judging our parents. When a man complains about his wife to us, we usually ask him, "What was your mother like?" It's amazing how many overweight wives have an overweight mother-in-law and how many alcoholic husbands have an alcoholic father-in-law! God's laws of sowing and reaping never fail, but the time and way in which they work are up to God.

Perhaps now you are seeing a similar pattern of trouble in your own life, marriage, or family. What is it? Is this pattern similar to something you saw in someone else? Did your husband become an alcoholic just like your father? Have you or your spouse become just like your father or mother in areas of bad behavior or character? Name them. Has your marriage fallen apart in similar ways to that of your parents'? Whom did you blame for these failures? Whom have you blamed and why? Perhaps some of these issues are immediately apparent. But if not, take a moment and ask God to show you any place where the law of judgment is negatively affecting you in the present.

What is Judgment?

We are now able to discover the underlying principles of judgment. Righteousness and justice are the foundations of God's governmental administration for His creation (Psalm 89:14). Judgment involves comparing someone or something against a standard of acceptance, quality, or

15

righteousness. When God judges, He has all the facts, including knowledge of what is/was in someone's heart (Proverbs 2:2). He weighs the attitudes and intent of a person's heart in His balance against the weights/standards of righteousness. He then deals with that person accordingly.

Unrighteous Judge vs. the Righteous Judge

Because we are usually unaware of judging others, many of us live in the land of adversity. Putting it simply, when we weigh and judge others, we are in sin; that is, we are unrighteous because of our judgments. Let's take a look at how we entered through the doorway of judgment into adversity and begin to look for a way of escape back through that door to the land of blessings and favor.

In Daniel 5, God writes on the palace wall that the king has been weighed in the balance (scales of God) and found deficient. When God does this weighing, He does it righteously and considers everything because He is omniscient. Jesus is the rightful Judge of all (Acts 17:31). But when we personally weigh and judge, there are four major problems:

- We may have some of the facts, but not all of them— i.e., we are not omniscient.
- We may not be self-aware, but from God's viewpoint we have our own prejudices and "blind spots" and therefore we are not impartial.
- We don't fully understand God's standards.
- In judging, we have pushed Jesus aside and taken His place as judge.

The functioning of the Law of Judgment is similar in principle to the Law of Forgiveness that we will look at in the next chapter. Supernaturally, trouble will come upon us for transgressing God's commandment. The Law of Judgment explains the legal punishment we will receive when we disobey Jesus' command, recorded for us by Matthew:

> *Do not judge so that you will not be judged.*
> *Matthew 7:1*

The apostle Paul echoes this command in his letter to the Romans, referring to all who pass judgment on others:

> *... in that which you judge another, you condemn yourself.*
> *Romans 2:1*

As Paul continues, he explains that while we may feel we are more righteous than those whom we are judging, actually, there are often areas in our lives where we are making the same kind of mistakes. The problem is that as we condemn others, we are, in effect, speaking the same judgment upon ourselves without seeing it. And Paul tells us that the judgment of God rightly falls on those (including ourselves) who practice these things. Jesus clarifies the issue as He explains just what will happen to us who judge others:

> *For in the way you judge, you will be judged; and by your standard of measure, it will be measured to you.*
> *Matthew 7:2*

As prayer counselors, my wife and I continually see the results of judging in people's lives. It is like a self-curse come true. The only escape is to renounce the judgment and ask God to forgive us for our words and for the internal score sheet that we've kept against the people whom we have judged. We can only be set free through the name of Jesus and by His precious blood, which not only opens the doors of heaven for us, but releases us from earthly captivity.

The following provides some model prayers to help you through the doorway of escape from the consequences of the Law of Judgment. This doorway of escape uses the only remedy possible, the blood of Jesus applied to your sin of judgment. In receiving Jesus as our Savior, we receive the right to enter eternity as a child of God; but through confession and repentance of sins, we are enabled to put the blood of Jesus over the doorways of trouble into our lives here on earth and escape that system of disfavor or curse. Please remember that your family, nation, or a group you may have belong(ed) to could have judged others in their history.

The best practice in prayers of release is to have a "Prayer Partner" stand with you for this process; i.e., have at least one other Christian witness your repentance and speak forgiveness, healing, and release to you in the name of Jesus. Of course, you can pray through the issues in this chapter on your own, just you and God, but we have provided scripted prayers for both you and a prayer partner to facilitate your passage from disfavor in life to favor.

Let's now use the following model prayer for each judgment issue that you have discovered.

Judgment: Stepping Through the Doorway of Release

Your Prayer and Declarations

Dear Heavenly Father, I now come to You in regard to my sin of judgment. I confess that I have judged (name of the person(s) or group) and have found (this /these persons or group) to be inferior or insufficient in my eyes, believing that I am superior to them and that I would not behave as badly or be like them if I was in the same position as they have been. Lord, this is the sin of judgment. I renounce this sin and choose by an act of my will to let go of this judgment in my heart. I proclaim that only You are the true judge. Therefore, I release (name the person(s) or group's name) to You for forgiveness or judgment as You see fit. Only You as God could know all the facts and conditions of their hearts to make the proper decision about their behavior. I now claim the shed blood of Jesus over my sin of judgment and ask that you would set me free from the consequences of this sin.

Prayer Partner Speaks*

In the name of Jesus, I speak forgiveness to you for your sin of judgment of (name of the person(s) or group) you are releasing in your heart. Lord Jesus, please help my brother/sister release his/her feelings over this issue to You. In the name of Jesus, I speak healing into your human spirit. Holy Spirit, please come and heal and comfort my brother/sister from all the wounds suffered in this issue into which we are now ministering.

*Please note that the Holy Spirit may bring up issues in this process that He wants to have uncovered—things that were, perhaps, not known. Listen and do what He says. Further, when commanding any spirits of curse to leave, watch to see what God is doing and give Him some time to bring about the cleansing and release. If possible, a process of restoration with the estranged parent/parents should be considered.

Chapter 3

The Third Doorway
It's Not What You Think It Is

Who's Responsible?

Most of us have those we hold responsible for some kind of adversity in our life, whether or not it is in our everyday awareness. If you can't think of anyone, consider this: many of us were hurt at an early age and have forgotten all about it. Perhaps you're wondering what that has to do with your life right now. Stay with us; it's a hidden doorway we're looking at, and how it works will be new to most, even to those who thought they understood about forgiveness.

We may or may not have said "I forgive." And even if we have said those words, the chances are that our forgiveness is not yet complete if we still have residual negative feelings about someone's actions. In this chapter we'll discover the way out of even the slightest bit of left-over unforgiveness. Forgiveness is one of the most misunderstood principles in the Bible and many Christians, even many pastors and church leaders, often do not have a full grasp of the concept as it applies to life on earth. Let's take a closer look.

The Hot Potato of Damage and Hurt

Unforgiveness comes from how people treat us or, better said, mistreat us. Someone does something unkind, or worse, to us, our automatic response is to be angry, to feel hurt, to be resentful, or to engage in some other form of unforgiveness. There are degrees and kinds of mistreatment:

- Physical damage and pain
- An unkind tone of voice when addressing us
- Demeaning actions towards us and words spoken to us or about us
- Un-thoughtfulness
- Shaming, embarrassing, humiliating, discrediting, dishonoring, defaming, disrespect
- Theft
- Violation of our rights, personhood, physical body, belongings, or someone dear to us, as well as our area, land or territory
- Withholding what is due and more

When someone damages or hurts us, it's like a burning hot potato is tossed into our hands: now what do we do? Often, our first reaction is to hit back, but instead we need to forgive, not throw the hot potato back at them. How can we do that? We have a *burning hot potato* in our hands, and we need to throw it somewhere, not just hold it and be burned by it saying . . . "It's OK!" So, where do we toss the potato? The answer, while simple, is not readily obvious. Let's look a little deeper.

Temporal and Eternal Effects of Forgiveness

Contemporary church teaching muddles up the belief in Jesus' work on the cross with interpersonal relationships. It's absolutely great that we can go to heaven (in eternity) when our body dies, because Jesus died for our sins. He paid the price for our entry in the heavenly realms—this concept is well understood by most Christians and churches in general.

But the problem is that we don't yet live in the heavenly realms in our day-to-day lives on planet earth. Our salvation experience doesn't answer what we do with the burning hot potato received when we're personally damaged. By now we know personal bad behavior earns us difficulty in this life (the word is "consequences"). So, returning hurt to those who damaged us will somehow negatively affect us. What, then, can we do? Forgiveness is the way out: but not the way we were taught growing up. The forgiveness principles we are about to explore can transfer some of the goodness from Jesus' sacrifice on the cross into situations where we've been hurt. It's an amazing way out of a very common but painful problem.

Let's look at a real-life example of applying these principles to gain new freedom. Ultimately, we're going to find out where to toss the burning hot potato of damage and hurt.

Real-Life Story

We had the following experience in a church setting, which illustrates one way the Law of Forgiveness might work in a person's life.

A young woman missionary came up to us for prayer at the end of a church service. She was suffering with a large tumor on one of her ovaries, which was causing her much discomfort. Her doctors had informed her that she needed immediate surgery, as it was developing into a life-threatening situation.

We began to pray for her, right there in the church. God gave me some questions to ask her that began to unwind the bonds of infirmity holding her in sickness. Our dialogue and prayer went something like this: "Tell me about your self-esteem. Do you like yourself?" A deep hurt began to surface as she took these issues to the Lord for His help to deal with them. The presenting symptom was a life-threatening tumor but attached to this physical condition were low self-esteem and a dislike of self. As we asked God to show us the root of this problem, she remembered an unresolved childhood issue of sexual abuse by a family member. This act severely devalued her and led to self-hate.

Finally, the root of unforgiveness towards her abuser had to be faced. In this case, as she released (forgave) her abuser to Jesus for judgment or forgiveness, she also expressed all her anger and pain to Him, telling Jesus just how she felt. The effect was immediate and dramatic: she was released from the self-hate arising from Satan's accusation that she was responsible for being abused. Self-hate had invited the tumor to grow.

As self-hate left her life, the enemy had no more rights to maintain the tumor. When she returned to the doctor a few days later to review her surgery options, the tumor was discovered to have reduced in size so dramatically that she no longer needed surgery.

The self-hate and retained anger living in this young woman's unforgiveness tormented her emotionally and physically, resulting in a life-threatening affliction.

24

The pain drove her to Jesus and His answer to her problem, as it is so clearly seen in the Law of Forgiveness. With understanding came a change of heart. She was set free through forgiving her attacker and being forgiven herself for her sin of unforgiveness.

Unforgiveness can often lead to judgment as we begin to denigrate the character and personality of the person who damaged and offended us. Let's explore this concept further in the next section.

The Law of Forgiveness

Just as there is a law of gravity, there is a law of forgiveness, but how to use it takes a little explaining:

> *... if you forgive men when they sin against you, your heavenly Father will also forgive you. But if you do not forgive men their sins, your Father will not forgive your sins*   *Matthew 6: 14-15 NIV*

Not only is this a spiritual law, guideline, or principle; but if we look closely, it is a doorway to the land of disfavor. Unforgiveness results in God holding things against us; it is certainly a curse. At the end of Matthew 18, Scripture reveals even heavier consequences to unforgiveness. Jesus tells a story about a man who refused to forgive someone. As He finishes, Jesus explains that when we willfully refuse to forgive others, God removes His protection around us and turns us over to demonic torturers, giving them free access to us until we change our mind and forgive.

So, let's examine some of the elements contained in the story above to see if we can recognize unforgiveness in our life and the lives of others. We will also learn how to escape the curse of unforgiveness. Our personal well-being depends upon our understanding and actions regarding unforgiveness!

The Dynamic of Personal Damage

In the previous real-life story, as a girl the young woman suffered humiliation, violation, defilement and then accusation that the violation she suffered was her fault. To understand why she was forgiving someone, she first had to have an idea of the damage or loss that she had sustained.

In general, when someone hurts or damages us, several things happen.

- First, we feel the damaging impact (i.e., the hurt that happened to us).
- Second, we have reactions—feelings of loss, pain, hurt, embarrassment, etc.
- Third, we desire justice—wherein the one who hurt us should suffer, perhaps even more than we have suffered.

Holding on to the second and third items is what gets us into trouble. In our heart, we hold the perpetrator responsible for his or her action. We may be angry and want to hurt the person in return; this intention is called vengeance. In the example, the young woman began to judge her attacker, even though she did not know what brought him to such a deed. But God requires us to release the matter (and persons) into His hands. It is God's job to

26

bring your claim of injury into the heavenly courts to weigh the matter and execute any punishment required.

Therefore, thus says the LORD,

"Behold, I am going to plead your case
And exact full vengeance for you ..."

Jeremiah 51:36

When we hold on to a matter (the pain, the accusation, and the desire for vengeance), we are in violation of the Law of Forgiveness: Through our unwillingness to let go, we enter through the doorway into the land of curse. While we may think that we understand everything about our being damaged, our knowledge is truthfully incomplete; only God knows and understands the whys and intents of heart. We are not to handle the matter other than to release it to Jesus. Forgiveness is not a feeling but a legal action, turning the matter over to God rather than our trying the case and executing our own justice. Our pain, distorted vision, and personal sense of righteousness do not qualify us to match Jesus' ability as the mediator of righteousness and justice.

You may ask, "What about the pain, loss, hurt, embarrassment, etc.?" These things we must give to Jesus immediately following the injury so that He can comfort us. Emptying our heart of the pain and hurt is part of the process of forgiveness; it makes room for God's comfort and healing and helps us to stop blaming, fault-finding, and accusation. Without the fuel of pain and unexpressed (internalized) emotions, the fire of our desire for vengeance will go out and it will be easier to trust God for His justice.

But if I forgive someone, won't I open myself up to more hurt?

Forgiving someone does not mean that we must trust them in their areas of weakness, the places where they have not changed. In forgiving, we have released our claim of revenge to Jesus. It does not mean that the person who hurt us has been processed or changed through our personal transaction with God. There is a huge difference between being forgiven and being trustworthy.

In the Law of Forgiveness, we are introduced to the concept that our rewards and punishment come from the heavenly realm, based upon what we do or think in the earthly realm.

For many of us, we are so earthly bound in materialism, science, history, medicine, psychology, and even traditional religion that we never consider the possibility that earthly suffering could be a manifestation of the spiritual consequences of our earthly behavior. In many churches, the primary focus has been evangelism because of the need for salvation leading to eternal life. But those who have been converted and added to our church have needs and problems in their lives that have spiritual origins. Many of their difficulties are a result of others sinning against them. Lack of forgiving the wounds and betrayal they have suffered is very often a key issue. One of the major difficulties that both Christians and non-Christians alike face is unforgiveness towards those who have hurt them. Let's now take a look at the doorway of escape from the land of adversity to the land of blessings and freedom.

Unforgiveness: Stepping Through the Doorway of Escape

The first step in obtaining freedom from this curse is to recall or discover any places where you or anyone in your direct bloodline, or any group to which you or your family belong(ed), were involved in unforgiveness. This process may involve praying for the Holy Spirit to remind you of your own retained anger, bitterness and unforgiveness. You may also need to ask members of your family about retained anger, bitterness and unforgiveness in the family line. Please remember that your nation or a group you belong to may have unforgiveness in their history.

The best practice in prayers of release is to have a "Prayer Partner" stand with you for this process; i.e., have at least one other Christian witness your repentance and speak forgiveness, healing and release to you in the name of Jesus. Of course, you can pray through the issues in this chapter on your own, just you and God, but we have provided scripted prayers for both you and a prayer partner to facilitate your passage from disfavor in life to favor.

Your Prayer and Declarations

Dear Heavenly Father, I come to you in the precious name of Jesus. I confess and turn from my sins of unforgiveness towards (name the offenders) for (name the offenses). Lord, I now give you all the hurt, pain, embarrassment, shame, and loss etc. ... I also now release all the bitterness, judgment, anger, and hatred that I was still harboring in my heart, giving it all to you. I release the whole matter to you to vindicate me, comfort me, and bring the whole issue to your perfect resolution.

29

I also come to you with these same things that have
been in my family (and/or group to which I belonged).
I choose by an act of my will to forgive (name the
persons or groups) for (the unforgiveness, retained
anger, bitterness, hatred, and judgments) by which they
opened the doors of curse into my life. I renounce
these beliefs and practices in the name of Jesus. I give
you any of this anger, bitterness, hatred, and judgment
that found a place in my life.

Heavenly Father, I also renounce and repent of the
unforgiving practices of my nation and all instances
where they retained bitterness, hatred, judgment, and
anger, particularly towards people groups.

Lord, I now ask you to forgive me in the name of Jesus
for these sins of unforgiveness. I claim the shed blood
of Jesus over these sins.

Prayer Partner Speaks*

I witness the confession, repentance, and prayers of
(your name) in regard to unforgiveness. In the name of
Jesus, I speak forgiveness to you for you and your
family's named sins of unforgiveness. In the name of
Jesus and through His precious shed blood, I release
you from the curses of the law of forgiveness. I
command any and every spirit present to carry out
these curses to leave (your name) right now in the

---

*Please note that the Holy Spirit may bring up issues in this process that
He wants to have uncovered—things that were, perhaps, not known.
Listen and do what He says. Further, when commanding any spirits of
curse to leave, watch to see what God is doing and give Him some time
to bring about the cleansing and release. If possible, a process of
restoration with the estranged parent/parents should be considered.

name of Jesus. I now speak healing, release, and restoration from the effects of these curses.

Holy Spirit, I ask that you now come and comfort (your name) in these places of damage and pain. Lord, would you please begin the process of restoration for every loss encountered from the damages inflicted.

Now, Holy Spirit, please come and cleanse and refill (your name) with Your presence in every place of damage and defilement. Please come and renew (your name's) mind in these areas where unforgiveness, bitterness, judgment and hatred were strongholds.

The Fourth Doorway
The Unworthy Parent(s)

This chapter may be difficult for some people, depending upon what kind of parents you had while growing up. As you read, you may find yourself peaceful, extremely agitated, or even incensed over the subject matter. But if it makes you angry, your anger could be an alarm bell ringing loudly that something is amiss. Maybe you are lacking in prosperity, sick and infirm, or facing less obvious forms of trouble. Much as you don't want to believe the root problem comes from your relationship with your parents, it may very well be so. Let's see if God has a great big blessing waiting for you as we investigate further.

Real-Life Story

Sarah could hardly believe her "good luck." She had been suffering with TMJ (temporomandibular joint syndrome) pain and paralysis in her jaw to the point that it was beginning to affect her job in sales. She was experiencing greater and greater stress in her life, so her boss at work referred her to a kind, well-respected psychiatrist who headed up the whole psychiatric wing of the local hospital.

On her first visit to his private practice, the psychiatrist asked a simple question: "Tell me how you feel about your father." "That's easy, I hate him!" she replied. "He secretly abused me from age three to thirteen when I was finally big and strong enough to stop him.

Even after I got married, he would call me in a drunken stupor after the bars closed and speak in unbelievably immoral ways to me. Not only was he that way in my childhood, but he has continued verbally to intrude into my life even to this very week! Sometime in my childhood, my mother discovered what he had been doing, but she did not protect me from him."

Sarah was one of those who received salvation as a child, but later as an adult received a "born-again" experience (see the Appendix). As she began to pursue God in this empowered condition, she became more aware of the fifth commandment:

> *"Honor your father and your mother, that your*
> *days may be prolonged in the land which the*
> *LORD your God gives you.*
>
> *Exodus 20:12*

"Just how could God put such a difficult requirement on me?" she wondered. "Surely, He knows how despicably my father has acted and continues to trouble me even to this day."

While the psychiatrist quickly got to the root of her problem, psychology could not heal her; ultimately it was prayer ministry as outlined later in this chapter that completely released her from the TMJ and a number of other life problems that came from the same source. The two main roots of Sarah's afflictions were unforgiveness (Chapter 3) and dishonoring her parents.

Many of us have suffered at the hands of our parents, what they did or did not do for us—not protecting us, giving us up for adoption, attempting to abort us, shaming us, not providing for us, neglecting us, abusing us, favoring a brother or sister above us, not loving us. So, what is the solution to this dichotomy: If God truly loves us, then how could He ask us to honor what seems to be the very source of our hurt, pain, damage, and rejection? It is a very good question, the answer to which we may never have thought possible.

Let's read on.

Honor

A good place to begin investigating the above commandment would be to look at the word *honor* as we understand it today and its usage in the ancient Hebrew where it was both spoken and written in God's Word.

Contemporary Usage

Today in common usage *honor* incorporates two concepts: reverence and deference, both of which imply yielding or submitting to another's judgment or preference out of respect for their position, abilities, or experience. As children, in honoring our parents we yield to their position of authority and guardianship over our life and our wishes to please them out of love. However, when our parents have not exercised that authority justly, and/or when they have not protected and nurtured us, we tend to distrust, rebel, and become disobedient. In more severe cases of neglect, abuse, and failure to protect, we may grow to hate and dishonor our parents, as was the case with Sarah in our opening example for this chapter.

Biblical Usage

In Exodus 20:12, the Hebrew word translated into honor is Strong's Word 3513: כָּבֵד *kāb ēd:* a verb meaning to weigh heavily, to be heavy, to be honored, to be made heavy (on your heart), to get honor, to make dull, to let weigh down, to harden, to multiply. Hebrew has fewer words than English and many words are understood by their context rather than having a specific, stand-alone meaning. We can, however, understand the meaning from other Scriptures; for example, Leviticus 19:3 from the pen of Moses and Matthew 15:4 from the mouth of Jesus.

> *Every one of you shall reverence his mother and his father, and you shall keep My sabbaths; I am the LORD your God.*
>
> *Leviticus 19:3*

> *For God said, 'HONOR YOUR FATHER AND MOTHER,' and, 'HE WHO SPEAKS EVIL OF FATHER OR MOTHER IS TO BE PUT TO DEATH.'*
>
> *Matthew 15:4*

In re-examining the fifth commandment, Exodus 20:12, we discover that there is a consequence for disobeying the command to honor: you will not be able to live in the land of God's blessings and your life will end earlier than would otherwise be expected. The negative rewards are not telling you what might happen, as in the first part of the verse, but rather they are a statement of truth. We are admonished to honor, but the consequence of not honoring in regard to our parents is a loss of privilege and an early death. In this verse, we discover that our sustenance in blessings and healthful life support will be diminished. The fifth commandment, then, is a health and welfare advisory just as much as a hurricane warning would be to the residents of a tropical island.

Historical Context

The *Ten Commandments* were given by God to the Israelites during their time of travel to the Promised Land. They had just left 400 years of slavery in Egyptian captivity (immersed in and adapted to an immoral culture) and were not particularly sensitive to God's ways and His heart's wishes. While they were to be the inheritors of lands promised to Abraham, the father of the Jewish nation, spiritually they were like children. Therefore, they were being trained by God as a parent trains his children. God gave them instructions to prepare them to enter the Promised Land. The *Ten Commandments* were parental in nature, designed to protect the children of Israel until such time as they knew better how to behave and to seek after God. Even Moses, their leader, who was trained in the courts of the pharaoh, realized he was not that far ahead of his subjects in knowing God, crying out to Him:

> *"Now therefore, I pray You, if I have found favor in Your sight, let me know Your ways that I may know You, so that I may find favor in Your sight.*
>
> *"Exodus 33:13*

So, what could have been on God's heart when He issued the fifth commandment?

It has to do with how God designed this world to operate. You see, God designed the family as His preferred way to bring a child into this world, then to raise and prepare him or her to operate as a mature human being. Anything that

37

disrupts family comes against His avowed plans and intent for mankind and planet earth in general. So, if there is parental dishonor in children's hearts, cooperation in the family is reduced and God's plans for families in general are being resisted. Secondly, there is the issue that ultimately God chose your parents and the family name that you and they bear. He had high hopes that they would love and nurture you, that they would bring you into maturity ready to know, serve, and cooperate with Himself.

As you probably know, not everyone who has loving, nurturing parents turns out well. And conversely, not all difficult parents have children who end up failing. Good parents show us how to do things right, and not-so-good parents show us what not to do. How we turn out, in the end, is our choice. While some of us wish we had better parents, the truth is that we can be shaped into godliness by what we decide to emulate as well as by that which we choose to behaviorally reject. We are not to judge our parents for their performance since that is not our privilege. We are warned in Matthew 7 to stay clear of judging others because, spiritually, it enters us into being judged by the same standards.

> *Do not judge so that you will not be judged. For in the way you judge, you will be judged; and by your standard of measure, it will be measured to you.*
> *Matthew 7: 1, 2*

While it may be true that your parents did not do as well as they might have in your life (perhaps continuing on to this day), how they have behaved is between them and the Lord; you need to release their failures to Him. Our commandment is to honor them because of the position given them by the Lord, the position of being your parents, just as we are to honor those in overseeing us and those in governmental offices, although they may not do their job as we think they should.

Sarah's Story Continued

Let's return to the true story from the beginning of this chapter. Sarah, who did not initially like the Fifth Commandment, decided to honor what she could in her father and his parental position. In her now Christian life, both she and her husband decided to try to reach out to her father somehow, to be kind and understanding.

On one occasion, they invited him to dinner. In this time with "Dad," they discovered the horrible childhood he endured. While not excusing Dad's behavior, they came to understand the roots of his bad behavior and ignorance of right and wrong. In fact, they also came to understand how well he did in a number of areas of life for which he was totally unprepared, based on his upbringing. It became easier for both Sarah and her husband to honor "Dad." While he did not change in any measurable way, and protective boundaries needed to be maintained because of his character, they personally began to experience a new peace and spiritual growth as they honored what they could.

"Dad" was a lifelong unbeliever. As he neared death from cancer, he now felt honored and safe with Sarah, so he was able to express his fears of dying to his daughter. Through her wise understanding and newly founded honor towards her father, she was able to tell him about Jesus and help him enter into salvation shortly before his death. We believe that Sarah will see her transformed father in heaven where he is able to be everything he was created to be.

As I shared the draft of this chapter with the "real-life Sarah," she commented on two factors that she wanted to clarify. The first was that she made a decision, asking the Holy Spirit to help her be obedient by reminding her of memories of some good things her father did. Initially she could think of nothing to honor him for. As God brought good remembrances to her mind, shockingly, she realized that some of these very things actually helped shape her character in a positive way. The second thing that happened was her heart became open to see her father in a better light and have a love for him that she had never experienced before. As their relationship progressed, she also found that her love and intimacy with God the Father deepened and she enjoyed more personal peace and physical health. She had found the doorway to the land of blessing and entered in. Let's see if we can help you enter the same doorway that Sarah discovered.

Dishonoring Parents: Stepping Through the Doorway of Release

The first step in obtaining freedom from this curse is to recall or discover any places where you or anyone in your direct bloodline or any group to which you or your family belong(ed) were involved in dishonoring others, particularly parents. This process may involve praying for the Holy Spirit to remind you of your dishonoring your parents and the (possibly suppressed) retained anger, bitterness and unforgiveness that supported it. You may also need to ask your family about disrespect in parent/ child relationships, retained anger, bitterness and unforgiveness in the family. Please remember that your nation or a group you belong to may not have an honoring history.

The best practice in prayers of release is to have a "Prayer Partner" stand with you for this process; i.e., have at least one other Christian witness your repentance and speak forgiveness, healing, and release to you in the name of Jesus. Of course, you can pray through the issues in this chapter on your own, just you and God, but we have provided scripted prayers for both you and a prayer partner to facilitate your passage from disfavor in life to favor.

Your Prayer and Declarations

Dear Heavenly Father, I come to you in the precious name of Jesus. I confess and turn from my sins of dishonoring my (mother and/or father) and all the unforgiveness and judgments towards (my mother and/or father) for (name any offenses). These activities and attitudes have supported my dishonoring them. Lord, I now give you all the hurt, pain, perceived embarrassment, shame, loss, etc. I also now release all the bitterness, judgment, anger, and hatred that I was still harboring in my heart, giving it all to you. I release the whole matter to you, for you to forgive me, comfort me, heal me, and bring the whole issue to your perfect resolution.

I also come to you with these same things that have been in my family (and/or group to which I belonged).

I choose, by an act of my will, to forgive (name the persons or groups) for (the dishonoring, unforgiveness, retained anger, bitterness, hatred, and judgments) by which they opened the doors of curse into my life. I renounce these beliefs and practices in the name of Jesus. I give you any of these: anger, bitterness, hatred, and judgments that found a place in my life.

Heavenly Father, I also renounce and repent of the dishonoring, unforgiving practices of my nation and all instances where they retained bitterness, hatred, judgment, and anger, particularly towards people groups.

Lord, I now ask you to forgive me in the name of Jesus for these sins of unforgiveness and dishonoring. I claim the shed blood of Jesus over these sins.

Prayer Partner Speaks*

I witness the confession, repentance, and prayers of (your name) regarding dishonoring (his/her) parents. In the name of Jesus, I speak forgiveness to you for your and your family's named sins of dishonoring parents and having unforgiveness toward them. In the name of Jesus and through His precious shed blood, I release you from the curses of dishonoring parents and harboring judgment and unforgiveness toward them. I command any and every spirit present to carry out these curses to leave (your name) right now in the

*Please note that the Holy Spirit may bring up issues in this process that He wants to have uncovered—things that were, perhaps, not known. Listen and do what He says. Further, when commanding any spirits of curse to leave, watch to see what God is doing and give Him some time to bring about the cleansing and release. If possible, a process of restoration with the estranged parent/parents should be considered.

name of Jesus. [Wait a moment for God to do this.]
Repeat this last command for each sin area renounced.
Check with the Holy Spirit to be sure that any
deliverance that was necessary has taken place.] I now
speak healing, release, and restoration from the effects
of these curses. Holy Spirit, I ask that you now come
and comfort (your name) in these places of damage
and pain.

Lord, would you please begin the process of
restoration for every loss encountered from the
damages inflicted. Now, Holy Spirit, please come and
cleanse and refill (your name) with Your presence in
every place of damage and defilement. Please come
and renew (your name's) mind in these areas where
dishonoring, unforgiveness, bitterness, judgment and
hatred was a stronghold.

Chapter 5

The Fifth Doorway
No Problem - I've Got It

My Way*

There's something comforting about being in control. Somehow it seems safer when we are in charge, then we don't feel so vulnerable. But there is a downside.

Real-Life Story

It was Jordan's first trip to the Amazon River basin. His mission: translate the Bible into a new tribal language. As he entered the two-seat, dual-control Cessna to be ferried further out into the jungle, the bush pilot gave him instructions about the flight. "The dirt runway is quite short as it was carved out of the jungle with difficulty. To clear the trees at the end of the runway, first we must gain enough airspeed; then we can pull up over them. Don't be afraid as we approach the end. I will pull up at the last moment and we will make it."

The pilot revved the engine before releasing the brakes and soon they were screaming down the runway, heading for the trees. Closer and closer they came to the end, but the small aircraft was not yet as high as the treetops. It looked like certain death to Jordan, and he could stand it no more. He reached forward to the

*In this chapter, we are not talking about the dynamic of exercising proper leadership authority in a workplace, in an organization, or in a spiritual headship position.

copilot's controls before him and with a mighty heave
he pulled back on the control yoke. The plane nosed
up, stalled in its climb, but continued forward to crash
belly first into the tree line. The impact was like
thunder in Jordan's ears as the trees tore off the wings
and the fuselage plummeted, tail first, towards the
ground in one piece. Both Jordan and the pilot
survived, but not without injury.

Often, taking control to do it our way doesn't turn out so
well. Perhaps you've had a few "crashes" of your own.
Let's see how this chapter might touch your life.

Some folks seem, more often than not, to end up in charge
of situations and interactions with others. For some, it is a
lifestyle choice (subconsciously or otherwise), but always
putting ourselves in control can remove us from the favor
of God. We call this practice *self-sufficiency*. Let's take a
look at a passage of Scripture from Jeremiah 17 to see what
happens when we habitually trust in ourselves or others
rather than God.

> *Thus says the LORD,*
> *"Cursed is the man who trusts in mankind*
> *And makes flesh his strength,*
> *And whose heart turns away from the LORD.*
> *For he will be like a bush in the desert*
> *And will not see when prosperity comes,*
> *But will live in stony wastes in the wilderness,*
> *A land of salt without inhabitant.*
> *Blessed is the man who trusts in the LORD*
> *And whose trust is the LORD.*

For he will be like a tree planted by the water,
That extends its roots by a stream
And does not fear when the heat comes;
But its leaves will be green,
And it will not be anxious in a year of drought
Nor cease to yield fruit.

Jeremiah 17:5-8

Paraphrasing this passage in Jeremiah, we come to the following understanding:

1. When we go to others or to our own devices to cover what we believe we do not have, we effectively turn our hearts away from God as our Provider, Protector, and the Supplier of all our needs.
2. In this position, we become personally isolated, even if we seemingly have a large group of friends.
3. Even when God provides opportunities for prosperity, we will not recognize them. Therefore, we will not receive the blessings realized from taking those opportunities.
4. On the other hand, if we continually look to God for His pathway through life, if we continually trust Him for our well-being, then—despite personal problems and even in climatic or societal seasons of difficulty—we will prosper and be useful.

Sarah's Story Continued

Let's take another look at the life of Sarah, whom we met in Chapter 4, as she was struggling to honor her father. Finally, she managed, with God's help, to be able to honor him, even with all his shortcomings. But her childhood interactions with him helped shape a lifestyle of self-sufficiency. Let's see the results in Sarah's life. Although your life circumstances may be different from hers, you may have arrived in a similar place, a place from which God wants to rescue you.

Sarah's difficulties began early in life. Her father started sexually abusing her at age three. She was defenseless against these violations that were shrouded in the name of love. Lack of the ability to defend herself held her captive in this cycle of abuse until age thirteen. Then a day came when she was old enough, big enough, and mature enough to rise up in anger, to shout loudly at her father that what he was doing was wrong, that she didn't like it, and that she would no longer allow him to do it. To her absolute surprise, he stepped back and stopped. Never again did she have that problem with him. As a result, she perceived that anger had saved her. She began to experiment in other situations where she felt she was being taken advantage of or when she was fearful. And most of the time anger worked with people backing down from their positions that appeared to threaten her.

As Sarah continued to grow up, unknowingly she honed this anger response into a skill that seemed effective to her. The problem was that it also drove people away from intimacy with her because they never knew when it would be their turn to suffer the wrath of Sarah. For Sarah, it was just a defense mechanism. After she had "torn your head off" in anger to make herself feel safe, and after the siege was over, she would change back into the friendly, sweet, caring person that she normally was. But those on the receiving end of her wrath were traumatized and could not again enter into the relationship with intimacy.

As the years progressed, she slowly migrated from the land of God's blessings to the land of adversity. Sarah now lived in that spiritually predicted desert, a place without other inhabitants (close personal relationships) as described by Jeremiah.

Then Sarah rededicated her life to Jesus as her Lord and Savior. She was baptized of her own free will and began to bring her life into compliance with God's ways. Eventually she became aware she was using anger as a defense (self-sufficiency) mechanism. When she asked God to show her why she used anger this way, she was reminded of the traumatic event with her father. God showed her that she had made a childhood inner vow which said, "I am only safe when I protect myself." She repented of this lie, of letting it control her. She then chose to trust God, turning to Him as her protector instead of herself. She renounced her practice of using anger to keep her safe.

When Sarah stepped aside from this self-sufficiency coping mechanism, she saw God quickly come to her aid. This experience made it easier for the next trial. Sarah developed a new habit of running to God instead of to herself. She began to be less fearful of being vulnerable and more assured that God would be there for her.

Happily, we can report here that she now has more real friends and is blessed by God, weathering the storms of life in His boat, not her own.

Perhaps your story and the resultant defense mechanisms or methods for goal accomplishment are different from Sarah's. But our results will be similar when we begin to look to ourselves or others for protection, favor, or accomplishment. Here's a list of just a few lifestyle mechanisms that we may use that seemingly help us avoid the need for God in our lives:

Self-Sufficiency Life-Style Mechanisms

- Anger
- Confrontation and the intimidating questioning of others
- Lying, stealing, cheating and deception
- Superior attitude
- Clothing, grooming, fashion and jewelry above the level of others
- Housing and possessions above the level of others
- Domination, control, and intimidation
- Education with the goal of being/appearing more intelligent than everyone else
- Attainment (amassment) of money and wealth
- Martial arts and bodybuilding
- Alliances for favor or protection, including clubs (like Free Masonry), gangs, associations, corruption and political offices for personal benefit
- Reliance on our good looks, beauty or handsomeness

- Acting the victim, manipulation, gossip, and
  passive/aggressive behavior

This list is seemingly endless, but the criterion is: Are you
using one of these mechanisms? Or have you found another
way to sidestep reliance on God to obtain your desires in
life? If, in the final analysis, you are trying to be a self-
made or self-sufficient person, you are under the curses of
Jeremiah 17:5. You will not have close personal
relationships and may not be prospering at the level that
God wishes for you.

God's Way
The rewards of living God's way are set out in Jeremiah
17:7-8, as documented earlier in this chapter. We can find
many other promises from God as well when we read
further in the Bible. For example:

> *Trust in the LORD with all your heart*
> *And do not lean on your own understanding.*
> *In all your ways acknowledge Him,*
> *And He will make your paths straight.*
> *Do not be wise in your own eyes;*
> *Fear the LORD and turn away from evil.*
> *It will be healing to your body*
> *And refreshment to your bones.*
>
> *Proverbs 3:5-8*

> *Though youths grow weary and tired,*
> *And vigorous young men stumble badly,*
> *Yet those who wait for [trust in] the LORD*
> *Will gain new strength;*
> *They will mount up with wings like eagles;*

They will run and not get tired,
They will walk and not become weary.

Isaiah 40: 30-31

Amazing! We've discovered another hidden doorway:
Now let's see how you can overcome self-sufficiency in
order to escape from the land of adversity or from the brink
of disaster.

Self-Sufficiency: Stepping Through the Doorway to Reliance on God

The first step in obtaining freedom from adversity brought
on by self-sufficiency is to recall or discover any places
where you or anyone in your direct bloodline or any group
to which you or your family belong(ed) are/were involved
with these sinful practices. This process may involve
praying for the Holy Spirit to remind you and convict your
heart of any such places in your life, currently or in the
past, where you were involved in the sin of self-sufficiency.

You may also need to ask your family about their practices.
But be careful. Many families pride themselves on their
wealth, independence, and self-sufficiency; therefore, they
may be blind to the ungodliness of it. Please remember that
your nation of origin or the people group you belong(ed) to
may not have a righteous history in this regard.

The best practice in prayers of release is to have a "Prayer
Partner" stand with you for this process; i.e., have at least
one other Christian witness your repentance and speak
forgiveness, healing, and release to you in the name of
Jesus. Of course, you can pray through the issues in this

chapter on your own, just you and God, but we have provided scripted prayers for both you and a prayer partner to facilitate your passage from disfavor in life to favor.

Your Prayer and Declarations

Dear Heavenly Father, I come to you in the precious name of Jesus. I confess and turn from my sins of self-sufficiency and the practice of depending upon mankind (including my practices and trusting my attributes and abilities) rather than God for the outcome of my life experiences (name all specific instances that you can recall).

I also come to you with these same sins that have been in my family (name any family members and their practices of self-sufficiency that you are aware of, as well those of your nation/ people group to which you belong[ed]). I repent for their sins and practices; i.e., how they carried out self-sufficiency. I choose, by an act of my will, to forgive (name the persons associated with or groups) for using the mechanisms of self-sufficiency by which doors of curse were opened into my life. I renounce these practices in the name of Jesus. I give you any anger, bitterness, hatred, and judgments against those who opened these doorways into my life.

Heavenly Father, I agree to not continue to benefit from the things obtained from others that I did not deserve, which were obtained through the mechanisms and practices of self-sufficiency. Please show me any way you wish me to step away from any benefits received or adversity avoided through my manipulation of circumstances in the practice of self-sufficiency.

Lord, I now ask you to forgive me in the name of Jesus for these sins practiced by me, my family, and any groups I belonged to (including my nation). I claim the shed blood of Jesus over these sins.

Lord, by the power of Your Holy Spirit, please retrain me to trust You and to be pleasing to You in any area where I was trusting in self or mankind to bring me the benefits that You wish for me.

Prayer Partner Speaks*

I witness the confession, repentance, and prayers of (your name) in regard to the practices of self-sufficiency. In the name of Jesus, I speak forgiveness to you for your and your family's named sins of self-sufficiency. In the name of Jesus and through His precious shed blood, I release you from the curses associated with self-sufficiency. I command any and every spirit engaged to carry out these curses to leave (your name) right now in the name of Jesus. [Wait a moment for God to bring this release. Repeat this last command for each sin area renounced. Check with the Holy Spirit to be sure that any deliverance that was necessary has taken place.] I now speak healing, release, and restoration from the effects of these curses.

*Please note that the Holy Spirit may bring up issues in this process that He wants to have uncovered—things that were, perhaps, not known. Listen and do what He says. Further, when commanding any spirits of curse to leave, watch to see what God is doing and give Him some time to bring about the cleansing and release.

Now, Holy Spirit, please come and cleanse and refill (your name) with Your presence in every place of damage and defilement through these practices. Please come and renew (your name's) mind in these areas where self-sufficiency was a stronghold. Holy Spirit, I ask that you now come and assist (your name) in the process of beginning to trust in the Lord rather than in self or in others to influence their life situations.

I pray that You, Lord, would now bring restoration. Please show Yourself faithful to (your name) and help (him/her), by Your Holy Spirit to learn to trust and to enter into a partner relationship with You to fulfill any deep needs which he/she tried to satisfy by themselves.

Chapter 6

The Sixth Doorway
My Hand Is Stuck in the Cookie Jar

Satisfaction, Relief, and Comfort

There is a fable about a small boy secretly raiding a cookie jar whom his mother caught because of his desire for more. The cookie jar had a somewhat smaller opening than its lower part, which led to the boy's hand getting stuck when he grasped a large handful. He could have withdrawn his hand if he had been willing to release some of the cookies. But with fingers outstretched, holding unto as many cookies as he could grasp, his hand could not be withdrawn through the narrower opening. Of course, he could have been free in a moment. But he loved the cookies and the delight/comfort that they gave him.

Some of us are like that little boy in that we are somehow stuck trying to get comfort and satisfaction from something we thought we wanted, or something that gives us some kind of momentary relief from life's problems. But what if using food, alcohol, drugs, or smoking to obtain comfort had a spiritual effect and were actually some of those hidden doorways to adversity?

A Shocking Discovery

The opening story of this chapter leads us into a surprising, more broad-brush definition of idolatry that includes how we use the things of this world. This chapter is so transforming, but simple, that you may want to re-read this section a couple of times: It will take away the power of addictions. Okay, that was a conclusion, but let's read on to discover why we said that.

In Chapter 9, we will examine idolatry from the perspective of worshiping other gods. When we look at idolatry in Chapter 9, we will find that false religions are practiced in the hope of gaining peace, welfare, comfort, and reward. In a false religion, we're told, if we just follow certain practices, we will receive the promised results by adhering to their doctrine. And, of course, worshiping other gods is the fundamental definition of idolatry. It fits our contemporary, surface understanding of the word idolatry.

But when we examine substances or activities that comfort and reward us, we can discern that they may also fall under the definition of idolatry. If we are going to something other than the living God for comfort, peace, and reward to receive what He wants to give us, we are also in idolatry. From this understanding, we get the functional definition of idolatry:

The Functional Definition of Idolatry:
Going to something other than God to get what He wants to give us

---

While it is clear that false gods and religions are idolatrous (see Chapter 9 for a more complete discussion), we can now begin to see that the use of ordinary earthly things or practices to get what God wants us to have is also idolatrous. These substitute things we use or engage in to get peace, comfort or safety can have a hidden spiritual power to take us through doorways to adversity that we would never have guessed.

We get our hands caught in the cookie jar because nothing but God will ever satisfy, as we try to get all the peace, comfort, or satisfaction possible. But we have gone to another source. While we may not have worshiped or served in a false religion to make us idolaters, let's take a look at the following activities, practices, and lifestyles that may match our new broad-brush, *functional* definition of idolatry.

Substance Abuse—*Tobacco, Alcohol, Narcotics, Food*
Going to food, cigarettes, alcohol or narcotics for comfort or peace is idolatry. It is difficult to stop using these "comforters" because they have the hidden spiritual power of idolatry, holding us in captivity in the land of adversity. But God is the God of all comfort; the Holy Spirit is the Comforter (John 15:26). Jesus is the Prince of Peace (Isaiah 9:6).

Substance abuse also leads to physical death as our bodies were not made to endure these things long-term or in great intensity. So, the wrongful use of these substances tears down our body, leading to the sin of self-murder!

A Process or Activity–
If the goal of participating in any activity is primarily to bring comfort or peace to areas of our lives that are anxious, in pain or in stress from past or present difficulties, there is a high probability this activity is idolatrous.

One such idolatrous practice is masturbation. Most
Christians, by the conviction of the Holy Spirit, realize that
masturbation is wrong. If you are engaged in this self-
comforting process, it is something you probably do in
secret. If you feel it's not socially acceptable and you do it
in secret, it should be a clue that it is a sin. The problem is
that the church has not addressed this issue very well since
there is no specific Scripture mentioning masturbation. But,
foremost, it is the sin of idolatry. Those engaged in this
practice find it difficult to stop because it has the hidden
spiritual power of idolatry.

Some time ago we were counseling a young woman who
asked us if masturbation is wrong. While we felt that it
was, we didn't know what to tell her. Desperately we cried
out to God in silent prayer for the correct answer.
Immediately He told us that indeed it is wrong and that it is
the sin of idolatry. It is comforting oneself rather than
coming to God for the comfort and peace that He wants to
bring us.

There is a further sin problem in masturbation. Most people
visualize/imagine a partner of the opposite sex while
performing this act. This practice also brings us into the
related sin of pornography, which involves physical
images. The Bible tells us that even looking at others to
whom you are not married, with the imagination of having
sex with them, is the same as adultery (see Matthew 5:27,
28). So there are at least two sin areas in this activity:
idolatry and adultery.

Materialism

If having or obtaining things or money begins to overshadow our relationship with God, our spouse, or our family, we need to examine what is happening to see if we are meeting a need within ourselves that God wants to resolve. We could easily be engaging in idolatry. The secondary sin in this area is the wrongful spending of time and money to the detriment or neglect of our families (both personal and church) to whom we have responsibilities, as commanded by God.

Work

Much like substance abuse, being a "workaholic" can also be a means of comforting ourselves or bolstering our self-worth (particularly if we've had low self-esteem). Work itself is, of course, something God wants us to engage in as part of personal responsibility. However, if we find ourselves spending all our waking hours working to the detriment of relationships with others and God as a way to ignore our feelings or comfort ourselves, it's a sure sign that work and its rewards have become an idol to us.

Person or Group

It is also possible to make an idol of our spouse, children, family, university, job, or favorite sports team. The test for all these possible "idols-in-disguise" is always the same. Are they displacing God in our attention and are we going to them in place of God to satisfy our needs? If we are, then we need to renounce this sin, confess it as idolatry, and cry out to God for forgiveness through the blood of Jesus.

Escaping the Fleshly Idols of Life: Stepping Through the Doorway to Freedom and Relief

This chapter is meant to sweep a little more broadly through your life to help you discover where you are not trusting God to supply all your needs. These are areas of your soul where something has taken the place of God in bringing peace, comfort, satisfaction, importance, prestige, material goods, safety, relationships—places where you have made flesh your strength (Jeremiah 17:5). When we depend upon something/someone other than God to meet our needs, that substitute may in effect have become an idol.

The best practice in prayers of release is to have a "Prayer Partner" stand with you for this process; i.e., have at least one other Christian witness your repentance and speak forgiveness, healing, and release to you in the name of Jesus. Of course, you can pray through the issues in this chapter on your own, just you and God, but we have provided scripted prayers for both you and a prayer partner to facilitate your passage from disfavor in life to favor. The prayer ministry that corresponds to your discovery of idols in your life is as follows.

Your Prayer and Declarations

Dear Heavenly Father, I come to You in the Name of Jesus and confess the sin of idolatry through the use of alcohol, narcotics, tobacco, masturbation, comfort eating, materialism, money, etc. By an act of my free will, I renounce this pathway to comfort, peace, safety, confidence, etc., that I was receiving from this process, substance, substitute for God. Holy Spirit, I ask that

You would help strengthen me not to use this substitute for God and His provision again. I agree that substance abuse and overeating shorten human life. Therefore, I confess the sin of self-murder (shortening my life) and ask that You would forgive me for this. I claim the shed blood of Jesus between me and this sin. By an act of my free will, I choose to forgive myself for this practice.

Prayer Partner Speaks*

In the name of Jesus, I speak forgiveness to you for the sins of idolatry that you just confessed. In the name of Jesus, I command every spirit of addiction, idolatry, and mockery from (name the idolatrous practice just confessed) to leave (your name) now. [Wait a moment for God to do this. Watch to see what happens and check with the Holy Spirit to be sure all deliverance necessary has taken place. Repeat this last command for each idolatrous practice renounced.] I command the spirit of (the) brand/product to leave (your name).

*Sometimes in substance abuse, it is important to renounce the favorite brand, e.g., cigarette maker, distillery name, or product name of the substance used.

Prayer Partner continues*

In the name of Jesus, I speak forgiveness to you for the

*Please note that the Holy Spirit may bring up issues in this process that He wants to have uncovered—things that were, perhaps, not known. Listen and do what He says. Further, when commanding any spirits of curse to leave, watch to see what God is doing and give Him some time to bring about the cleansing and release. If possible, a process of restoration with the estranged parent/parents should be considered.

sin of self-murder. [Look directly into their eyes and say the following:] I speak life to you in the name of Jesus. Now, in the name of Jesus, I command the spirits of death that came in through (name the sinful practice of substance abuse which the person has just renounced and repented) to go. [Wait a moment for God to do this. Check with the Holy Spirit to be sure that all deliverance that was necessary has taken place.]

Your Prayer continues:

[Where someone has helped you to begin or sustain these idolatrous habits, you will need to forgive them for leading you into or helping you carry out this sin, the following prayer would be appropriate.]

Dear heavenly Father, by an act of my free will, I now choose to forgive (name of the person/persons) who led me into this sin or assisted me in it for (his/her/their) part in my sin of (name the sin).

Prayer Partner continues:

Lord, please separate (your name) from (his/her) ungodly soul tie with (name of person/persons he/she was attached to through substance abuse). Jesus, please return everything of (your name's) life to (him/her) that was wrongly invested in (name of the person/persons with whom he/she was joined in the sin of idolatry) and release everything of (this/these) (person/persons) from your name.

Your Prayer continues:

[If you have confessed and repented of masturbation, the following prayer would be appropriate.]

Lord, I also confess the sin of adultery—looking on a picture or imagining someone with whom I would be having sex in my practice of masturbation. I confess this as adultery of the heart.

Prayer Partner continues:

In Jesus' name, I speak forgiveness to (your name) for his/her sin of adultery (of the heart) in the idolatrous practice of masturbation. I command every spirit of masturbation that has attached to (your name) to leave him/her now.

Chapter 7

The Seventh Doorway
Captured Eyes – Copied Practices

Captured by Our Eyes–Monkey See: Monkey Do

Many of us have been ambushed by movie makers, the media, and the worldly spirit behind them. Here is a common example where our eyes, imagination and hearts can be captured:

Real-Life Story

We had been watching the movie for a while. The action was superb, the plot was everything we could hope for, and the villains were certainly going to be vanquished by the hero and heroine fighting for justice and righteousness. It would not be long before the criminals would be behind bars. What's not to like? It is the subplot that gets us into trouble here.

The cinema-graphic sexual tension between the hero and the heroine had been built up by the movie makers throughout the movie with a question continually hanging in the air: Will they or won't they have unmarried sex before the movie is over? Finally, the evil men are brought to justice. The focus shifts to the hero and heroine ... at last, they kiss. The camera focus blurs a little while soft romantic music floods the soundtrack. Divesting themselves of clothes, they fall into bed together for unmarried sex.

We are being visually seduced by identification with the good characters for the purpose of getting us to mentally agree (in our hearts) with their sexual behavior. The good guy and good gal, after (or even perhaps during) their adventurous fight for righteousness, enter into unmarried sex. Many watchers of the film are caught up into hoping they "get together" sexually. Everything the movie makers set out to do moves our hearts. Our eyes and souls are successfully captured, lust is engendered and somewhere deep inside we feel justified in our own practices—or at least begin to feel—that it is okay to behave like the movie stars. The crime fighting hero and heroine are the good guys, so if it is okay for them, then we're enticed into thinking it is okay for us. We're ready to copy them, or perhaps justify our ongoing or previous same wrong practices.

But God's instruction manual, the Bible, clearly tells us that sex outside of marriage (adultery) will harm us. The first place in the Bible that the word adultery appears is in the *Ten Commandments*, Exodus 20:14, where we are told, "You shall not commit adultery. In Matthew 5:28, Jesus tells us that everyone who (*even*) looks at a woman with lust for her has already committed adultery (*in his heart*).

Doorways to Freedom
This seventh doorway to freedom can transfer a person from sexual sin—and its accompanying adverse results—to freedom and purity. Since this information is so diametrically opposed to the current social practices of much of the world, many of us have not understood that our own choices are causing us suffering.

Let's take a moment to remind ourselves about the theme of this book. We've discovered, in general, that there are many cause and effect principles not explained by the laws of physics, chemistry or engineering that we learn in school. These principles have an influence on our personal well-being. As we now can begin to discover, sexual sin is another one of the doorways to adversity. Let's read on to see how this is possible and discover if this doorway somehow touches your life.

The laws of sexual sin are not to be viewed as prudish or as punishment, but rather they are simple cause and effect principles explaining how our sexual behavior influences our well-being. If, while chopping wood with a hatchet we cut off our finger, we would expect it to be separated from our hand. It is not for punishment that our finger comes off; it is just a result of our behavior. It is obvious to most that this action would cause the expected result. But in this book, we are examining some not-so-self-evident principles to help bring you out of ignorant adversity and into the land of knowledgeable well-being. As an aid to understanding, let's look at a real-life story.

Real-Life Story

Harry Gordon Selfridge, born in Wisconsin, rose to fame and fortune through amazing vision and innovation ahead of its time while in his position at Marshall Fields, a Chicago department store. After selling his company stock options, he opened his first department store, under his own name, which later became Carsen Pierre & Scott in Chicago; but Selfridge soon sold it.

Taking his millions to London, he opened Selfridges Department Store on Oxford Street. He continued to prosper, multiplying his net worth into a fabulous fortune. But Selfridge had a sexual appetite that led him into unmarried sexual relationship after relationship. It can be argued that while his Christian wife, Rose, was alive, she helped keep him on the straight-and-narrow. However, following her death, it seems, he began to pursue sexual immorality in earnest.

After joining Freemasonry Lodge 2397 in London, Selfridge became sexually involved with Syrie Wellcome, the ex-wife of Henry Wellcome, a pharmaceutical multi-millionaire and founder of that Lodge. The affair, which lasted several years, ended badly. Harry then went on to become sexually involved with Lady Victoria Sackville, Gaby Deslys, Alice Delysia, Anna Pavlova, Elinor Glyn, Isadora Duncan, Marcelle Rogez, and finally the beautiful and famous twin Dolly sisters, who are regarded by many as his final downfall through sex and gambling. On each of these women, he lavished luxuries, expensive gifts, and money. Selfridge died alone, broken, and poor, having completely dissipated a vast fortune through his immorality![1]

Harry Selfridge reaped the consequences of choosing spiritual pollution instead of purity. If only he had been aware of God's instruction and heeded it, his life could have turned out differently. In Proverbs 5:3-11, Harry's

---

[1] Lindy Woodhead, *Shopping, Seduction & Mr. Selfridge* (New York: Random House, 2012).

downward trajectory was predicted in clear black and
white:

> *For the lips of an adulteress drip honey and smoother
> than oil is her speech; But in the end she is bitter as
> wormwood, Sharp as a two-edged sword. Keep your
> way far from her and do not go near the door of her
> house, or you will give your vigor to others And your
> years to the cruel one; and strangers will be filled with
> your strength And your hard-earned goods will go to
> the house of an alien; and you groan at your final end,
> When your flesh and your body are consumed;*
>
> *Proverbs 5:3-11*

The Truth about Sexual Sin

By now you might be wondering how some sex can be
wrong if sex is pleasurable and if we are not imposing our
will on someone else or breaking trust. Most of us are
aware of moralistic viewpoints held by certain members of
society, but today these don't seem to be held by the
general public. We all go to many of the same movies,
watch many of the same TV programs, and read the same
best-selling books.

But let's take a deeper look at what the Bible says about
this matter and discover some truths hidden in plain sight,
truths that may be affecting our everyday life and even our
future privileges in heaven (if hopefully we make it there)
after our body dies. You see, like the other doorways
between adversity and well-being, it doesn't matter if you
are religious or not or if you believe in God for this law to
affect you. It is just the way things were made; it is indeed
a spiritual, cause-and-effect law (principle). Let's discover

the truth about sexual behavior so you can decide for yourself and, if needed, pass through the doorway from adversity to freedom and favor, from pollution to purity.

All Sex Is Spiritual

Surprisingly, all sex has a spiritual element; it is not just physical. Most believe that it is just a bodily act, albeit one of intense physiological/emotional pleasure, that sometimes produces babies. We know that science has allowed us to circumnavigate the production of children and even the transmission of sexually transmitted diseases most of the time to seemingly get pleasure without consequences. But, since sex is also spiritual, and there is no such thing as a spiritual condom, we will discover: We cannot avoid its spiritual consequences, even if we don't initially see or sense them. It seems Harry Selfridge, a church goer who had a Christian wife, was blind to, ignorant of, or overlooked the spiritually induced dangers. But whatever his attitude or understanding, he succumbed to them anyway. Let's further examine this spiritual element.

God, who is a Spiritual Being, designed sex to be pleasurable, have spiritual aspects, and be the physical process leading to procreation; it is one package. What we have missed in our quest for consequence-free sexual pleasure is understanding the spiritual aspect. In having sex outside of marriage, we are standing against God's original plan for all of mankind. Standing against God's ways and wishes is sin and self-destructive. So, what is His plan for sex and what are the spiritual aspects?

Every time we engage in interpersonal sexual activity, either we create a spiritual bond/connection, or we

72

reinforce one that is already in place. In Genesis 2:24 this connection is documented:

For this reason, a man shall leave his father and his mother, and be joined to his wife; and they shall become one flesh.

Genesis 2:24

This spiritual connection, joining the husband and wife, making them one flesh (founding an invisible attachment between their souls), was not just for the moment of intercourse, but designed to be a conduit (connection) of spiritual nurture between the two individuals so joined. It was meant to be a lifelong supply line that does not disappear when the sex act is completed. Since it is a spiritual connection, it is not limited by time and earthly distance. If this connection is initiated within the covenant (commitment) of marriage, then love and nurture will flow both ways between the husband and wife.

If, however, the sexual/spiritual supply line is initiated outside of marriage, more than nurture can and will be transmitted, as it does not have the blessing and protection of God guarding it. It is a spiritual highway between the individuals that can carry anything, including curse and spiritual disfavor, from individual and family sins of the present and past. In either case the sexual act is a lifelong connection, whether established inside or outside of God's will, permission, and protection. The negative effects, those outside of God's will, are detailed in Proverbs 5:3-11 and describe what happened to Harry Selfridge in his sexual sin. In Proverbs 5:22 the consequences of these ungodly connections or ties regarding sexual sin are further detailed:

*His own iniquities will capture the wicked. and he will
be held with the (spiritual) cords of his sin.*

Proverbs 5:22

Sexual Sin Further Explained

Two key English language words describe sexual sin as
translated from the Bible: fornication and adultery.
Fornication is translated from the Greek word (Gr. πορνεία)
porneías and is generally understood as having sex with
someone to whom you are not married. Adultery is
translated from the Hebrew word (H. נָאַף) *nā'ap* and is
generally understood as having sex with someone you are
not married to, when either or both of the two participants
is married to another.

Some Old Testament Admonitions in Regard to Sexual Activities and Marriage

The following table, taken from the Pentateuch (the first
five books of the Bible), presents some admonitions that
were originally given to the people of Israel when they
came out from a pagan country (Egypt). They were
intended to shape the Hebrew people to be God's people,
reflecting His ways and being blessed as they obeyed Him.
His people needed to understand God's high standards and
the consequences of sexual sin. While the spiritual
consequences for these sins remain in both the temporal
and eternal realms today, God's social execution of justice
is no longer carried out. If some of these sins have been
committed by you or your family, you will be experiencing
some level of adversity. But the good news is: there is a
doorway to freedom in the next section.

Boundaries of Sexual Behavior

Sexual Partners Precluded	Reference	Consequence Named	Explained As
Your Father	Leviticus 18:6		
Your Mother	Leviticus 18:6		
Your Sister (Daughter of your parents – of either or both)	Leviticus 18:9 Leviticus 18:11 Deut. 27:21	Cursed	
Your Son's Daughter (Granddaughter)	Leviticus 18:9		
Your Daughter's Daughter (Granddaughter)	Leviticus 18:9		
Your Father's Sister (Aunt)	Leviticus 18:11		
Your Mother's Sister (Aunt)	Leviticus 18:11		
Your Father's brother's wife (Aunt)	Leviticus 18:14		
Your Son's Wife (Daughter-in-law)	Leviticus 18:14		
Your Brother's Wife (Sister-in-law)	Leviticus 18:14		
Woman and Her Daughter	Leviticus 18:17		Lewdness
Woman and Her Son's Daughter	Leviticus 18:17		Lewdness
Woman and Her Daughter's Daughter	Leviticus 18:17		Lewdness
May not marry a woman and her sister as a rival while they are both alive	Leviticus 18:17		
Any woman during her menstrual cycle	Leviticus 18:19		
Your Neighbor's Wife	Leviticus 18:19	You will be defiled with her	
A male as one lies with a female	Leviticus 18:22		Abomination
Any animal	Leviticus 18:22, Deuteronomy 27:21	You will be defiled with it Cursed	

Boundaries of Sexual Behavior

Sexual Partners Precluded	Reference	Consequence Named	Explained As
Any woman with an animal	Leviticus 18:22		Perversion
Another man's Wife	Leviticus 20:10	Both are to be executed	
Father's Wife	Leviticus 20:10	Both are to be executed	Blood-guiltness
Daughter-in-law	Leviticus 20:12	Both are to be executed	Incest
A male as one lies with a female	Leviticus 20:12	Both are to be executed	Detestable Act
Marrying a woman and her mother	Leviticus 20:14	Execution by fire	Immorality
Any animal	Leviticus 20:14	Both are to be executed	Blood-guiltness
Any woman with an animal	Leviticus 20:16	Both are to be executed	
Sister	Leviticus 20:17	Banished from nation	Disgrace
Menstrual sex	Leviticus 20:18	Cut off from their people	
Uncle's Wife	Leviticus 20:18	Will die childless	Abhorrent
Brother's Wife	Leviticus 20:18	Will die childless	Abhorrent
Mother-in-law	Deut. 27:23	Cursed	

From this table, we can see that God intended sexual activity to occur in marriage. But when it does not, when it is practiced outside of marriage, He says there are eternal consequences.

> *Fornicators and adulterers will not inherit the Kingdom of God (i.e., go to heaven).*
> *1 Corinthians 6:9*

Perhaps you never physically, sexually, cheated on your spouse, but Jesus says it is possible to commit adultery in our hearts without ever having sex.

But I say to you that everyone who looks at a woman with lust for her has already committed adultery.

Matthew 5:32

The Bible is quite direct about sexual sin in both the Old and New Testaments. The preceding table reveals Old Testament consequences when sexual relationships outside marriage violate God's directives. When God first gave these directives, He was bringing the Israelites into compliance with His plans to be His people, representing Him on the face of the earth. In these directives, God did not want the attractiveness of sexual sin to pollute the nation that He was forming: Therefore, He prescribed the death penalty on many forms of these sexual sins.

While these admonitions against sexual sin were first given thousands of years ago to the nation of Israel, they have never been rescinded: They are the standards that the God of Israel has for those who would worship Him. Further, they are the standards for those living on His creation, planet earth. You can expect adversity to be present in your life, even today, for living outside of God's ways.

Sexual Sin: Stepping Through the Doorway of Release from Sexual Sin

The first step in obtaining freedom from the curses associated with these sins is to recall or discover if you or anyone in your direct bloodline was involved in sexual sin.

This process may involve praying for the Holy Spirit to remind you of any family stories you may have heard. You may also want to ask your family about this matter. Since some level of shame and embarrassment may be involved, there is often secrecy, and with the passage of time it is possible that the actual sin may not be remembered or documented. Don't worry—all is not lost if you don't have information on your family. (We'll handle this possible lack in the next section.)

Another hindrance to freedom is that many of us have had a number of sexual partners outside of marriage. It is important to pray through the prayers of release for each of our sexual sins. When the number of partners is more than three or four, you may have to ask the Holy Spirit to remind you of their names or the time, location, or circumstance of the transgression to identify each one. When there have been many, it is best to pray about it and make a list before starting toward the doorway of release

The best practice in prayers of release is to have a "Prayer Partner" stand with you for this process, i.e., have at least one other Christian witness your repentance and speak forgiveness, healing, and release to you in the name of Jesus. Of course, you can pray through the issues in this chapter on your own, just you and God, but we have provided scripted prayers for both you and a prayer partner to facilitate your passage from disfavor in life to favor.

Your Prayer and Declarations
*For the Direct Bloodline Family**

Dear Heavenly Father, I come to you in the precious name of Jesus. I confess and turn from the sexual sins of those in my direct bloodline whose sexual sin is known (name the persons) and of anyone else in my family who was sexually involved in fornication, adultery, or other sexual sin outside of marriage. I renounce and repent of this practice in my family. I release them into the freedom of my forgiveness for bringing this influence into my life. I renounce all my judgments and unforgiveness towards my family for their sexual sins.

Prayer Partner Speaks
For the Familial Sins

I witness the confession, repentance, and prayers of (your name) regarding the familial practice of performing sexual intercourse outside of the boundaries of a committed, legal marriage in the name of Jesus. I claim the blood of Jesus between you and the familial sexual sins of fornication/adultery (and/or) other named sexual sins in your bloodline. In the name of Jesus, I release you from the influence of your family's named sexual sins. I speak forgiveness to you for your family's named sexual sins. In the name of Jesus and through His precious shed blood, I release you from the familial curses associated with fornication, adultery and other sexual sins. In the name of Jesus, I command every spirit associated with these sins to leave (your name).

*Where there is more than one known family member's sin, please name each person.

79

Your Prayer
*For Your Personal Sexual Sins**

I confess and repent of all my sexual sins, including adultery/fornication with (name the person/person's) and claim the shed blood of Jesus over my sin of fornication/adultery. I also include all other (name the sexual sins). I forgive myself and/or (name the partner) for bringing this sin into my life. I release the whole matter to you to forgive, cleanse, comfort, heal, and remove any curse associated with these sins from me. I renounce the pleasure that I received from these sexual sins. Lord, please release me from the one-flesh tie to this person that was initiated in sexual intercourse. I also choose, by an act of my will, to not treasure the memory and pleasure of this sin nor to reenact it in my mind (fantasize) to recall the details and pleasure of it. Holy Spirit, I did do this, but please help me to make this memory a forbidden place to dwell in self-comforting, pleasure, or satisfaction of any kind. Holy Spirit, I ask for your help to keep me from going to the pollution of these memories.

*In this prayer sequence include the name or identity for each person with whom you had sex outside of marriage. While this process is time consuming, it is important to go through it for each sexual partner involved in fornication and or adultery, as the curses/afflictions and level of influence and control from each sexual partner varies by individual.

Prayer Partner Speaks*
For the Personal Sexual Sins

In the name of Jesus, I now speak forgiveness, to (your name) for your confessed and repented sexual sins, including fornication/adultery (and other named sexual sins). Lord Jesus, I ask that you would now release (your name) from the one-flesh soul tie to (named sexual partner), returning everything of (your name) to himself/herself and returning everything of (named sexual partner) back to himself/herself.

In Jesus' name, I now command every spirit that came upon (your name) from this sexual sin to leave him/her now.* Go in Jesus' name! [Wait a moment for God to do this. Check with the Holy Spirit to be sure that any deliverance that was necessary has taken place. Repeat this last command for each/any spirit/influence that the Holy Spirit brings up.] I now speak healing, release, and restoration to you from the effects of these personal curses. [Wait and watch to see what the Holy Spirit may be doing, giving Him some time to do so.] Now, Holy Spirit, please come and cleanse and refill (your name) with Your presence in every place of damage and defilement and curse. Please come and renew (your name's) mind, will and emotions in these areas.

---

*Please note that the Holy Spirit may bring up issues in this process that He wants to have uncovered—things that were, perhaps, not known. Listen and do what He says. Further, when commanding any spirits of curse to leave, watch to see what God is doing and give Him some time to bring about the cleansing and release.

Chapter 8

The Eighth Doorway
They Weren't Married

What Does It Matter?

If your parents were not married when you were conceived, you are not alone; worldwide, many share your beginnings, and contemporary society believes the child of unmarried parents is no different than anyone else. However, what is not understood by most are the spiritual consequences for those with this origin. Let's take a look at both contemporary secular and Biblical information to discover how you might be unknowingly suffering and to help you find the hidden doorway to a better life.

Common Condition of Millions

The information we are about to share with you is nearly unbelievable as to its extent in world-wide occurrence: a governmental office discovered something that God has proclaimed. Of course, the government didn't understand the spiritual implications. But let's read on to find out what they unearthed from their mountains of documents and then see how this information might help us in our search for spiritual doorways to a better life.

This mind-boggling story, amazingly, starts with the US Department of Immigration's charter to allow only "quality" persons to enter the United States for the purposes of becoming a citizen. Leaving no stone unturned in their pursuit of excellence, the Department examined the circumstances of a person's conception.[2] Here's where it becomes interesting: they looked at millions and millions of records for the whole nation and found, typically, there were some terrible circumstances suffered by those whose parents were not married at the time of their conception. It was discovered that illegitimate children (conceived out of wedlock) typically have a plethora of social problems: high rates of poverty, imprisonment, low academic achievement, and a higher probability of becoming unmarried parents themselves. The statistics show illegitimate children will have increased high school dropout rates, more conflict with the law, increased illegal drug use and welfare use in their family. Illegitimate infants have higher mortality rates; and if they live, they suffer from more-difficult-to-measure problems while growing up, such as low levels of self-esteem and self-worth. Further, these children are more likely to produce children conceived out of wedlock, perpetuating the cycle down the generation line. By now you may be thinking that illegitimacy sounds like a curse. If you were conceived out of wedlock, some of these circumstances may be affecting you. But stay with us, there is a doorway to a better life for you, and we are working our way there.

The World-wide Magnitude of Illegitimacy

God planned for each child born to be brought up in a stable loving home by parents committed to each other and

---

[2] Steven A. Camarota, "Illegitimate Nation: An Examination of Out-of-Wedlock Births Among Immigrants and Natives" (Washington, D.C. Center for Immigration Studies, June 1, 2007).

to their offspring who would be protected, nurtured, and developed to step into the life He has prepared for them. Increasingly, this type of quality upbringing is not possible as more and more are unmarried when they conceive children, and many of these unmarried parents never intend to make that lifelong commitment to each other, let alone take responsibility for raising, maturing, and launching their children into life. In most nations of the world, we can discover the parents of many children being born today are not married: they conceive their children before marriage.[3]

- As of 2014, in Chile, Costa Rica, Iceland and Mexico, nearly 70% of the children born were conceived out of wedlock.
- In France, Norway, Sweden, Belgium, Denmark, Portugal, and the Netherlands, the children conceived out of wedlock are between 50-60% of all births.
- In the United Kingdom, the percentage hovers near the 50% mark.
- In the United States, as of 2014, about 40%. (For the United States this statistic is an increase from less than 10% in 1964.)

Most countries in the world are showing similar or greater gains in illegitimacy. Worldwide, as of 2016, about 21 million children were conceived out of wedlock each year. Something is going on. It might be attributed to books, magazines, newspapers, movies, and television eroding worldwide society, but that's a story for another time!

---

[3] Joseph Chamie, "Out of Wedlock Births Rise Worldwide" (New Haven, CT: Yale Global Online, March 16, 2017), Retrieved from https://yaleglobal.yale.edu/content/out-of-wedlock-births-rise-worldwide.

The Curse of Illegitimacy

As we read this data with spiritual eyes, we cannot escape the conclusion that some level of curse is operating on those of illegitimate origin. If you are suspecting this conclusion is true, you are correct, but where is the documentation? In the Book of Deuteronomy, Moses records for us the curse of illegitimacy.

> *A person begotten out of wedlock shall not enter into the assembly of the LORD; even to his tenth generation shall his descendants not enter into the congregation of the LORD.*
>
> *Deuteronomy 23:2 Amp.*

When we examine the Center for Immigration Study along with the above Scripture in Deuteronomy, we can expect to see the following results from the curse of illegitimacy.

Difficulties Suffered by Illegitimate Children[4]

- Higher rate of poverty
- Lower level of academic achievement
- More likely to drop out of high school
- More run-ins with the law
- More illegal drug use
- More incidences of incarceration
- More familial welfare use
- Infants suffer higher mortality
- Lower self-esteem and self-worth
- More likely to conceive illegitimate children
- Increased chances of negative social outcomes

---

[4] Camarota, "Illegitimate Nation."

86

- Increased criminality
- Weak attachment to the labor force

Both the secular university and governmental studies have documented the lives of thousands of children with unmarried parents, giving us a great deal of statistical data. But, at the same time, God's ancient Biblical Law provides a spiritual cause and effect understanding of this phenomenon.

Let's see if we can discover anything further in Deuteronomy 23:2 from the Hebrew language in which this law was first recorded over three thousand years ago by Moses.

The first significant Hebrew word translated into English as out-of-wedlock in Strong's Concordance is number 4464: מַמְזֵר, *mamzēr:* It is a masculine noun that identifies an illegitimate child, a bastard. It specifies a person who does not have a proper pedigree or genealogy and was born (conceived) out of wedlock.

The second significant Hebrew word is assembly or congregation. In Strong's Concordance it is number 6951: קָהָל *qāhāl.* This word is used to describe Israel as a congregation, an organized community. Israel was the Lord's community.

With the understanding of these two words, we can better grasp the consequences of the "Law of Illegitimacy" stated in Deuteronomy 23:2, as they pertain to Israelites, in particular, and then to all others. In ancient Israel, anyone conceived out of wedlock and anyone in their family line (down to the tenth generation) was to be excluded from membership privileges and benefits promised by God to citizens of the nation. With this statutory command of social ostracism, the individual and those following in their bloodline would be outcasts: They would develop, in their personalities and lifestyles, their reactions to rejection. Now we can begin to understand why illegitimate individuals and families of today tend to be social outcasts and end up displaying characteristics like the contemporary life templates discovered by the US Department of Immigration.

Illegitimacy: Stepping Through the Doorway of Illegitimacy to Release

The first step in obtaining freedom from this curse is to recall or discover if you or anyone in your direct bloodline were conceived out of wedlock. This process may involve praying for the Holy Spirit to remind you of any family stories you may have heard and even checking marriage and birth records. You may also want to ask your family about this matter. Since the roots of this curse can go back ten generations, it is possible that the actual sin may not be remembered or documented. Don't worry, all is not lost if you don't have information on your family. We'll handle this possible lack in the next section.

The best practice in prayers of release is to have a "Prayer Partner" stand with you for this process, i.e., to have at least one other Christian witness your repentance and speak forgiveness, healing, and release to you in the name of Jesus. Of course, you can pray through the issues in this chapter on your own, just you and God, but we have provided scripted prayers for both you and a prayer partner to facilitate your passage from disfavor in life to favor.

Your Prayer and Declarations

Dear Heavenly Father, I come to you in the precious name of Jesus. I confess and turn from the sin of anyone in my direct family bloodline who conceived children outside of wedlock. I renounce any practice of this in my family. [If this is also your personal sin—I repent of this practice of conceiving children, (name the persons if they are known to you). If your parents were not married before your conception—I forgive my father and mother for conceiving me outside of wedlock.] I renounce all my judgments and unforgiveness towards my mother and father for conceiving me outside of wedlock.

Lord, I now give you all the hurt, pain, perceived embarrassment, shame, and loss, etc. I also now release all the bitterness, anger, and hatred that I was harboring in my heart, towards them; I give it all to you. I release the whole matter to you to forgive me, comfort me, heal me and remove this curse from me. [If you conceived children outside of wedlock, I also ask you now to lift the curse of illegitimacy from my child/children in Jesus' name.]

Lord, I now ask you to forgive me in the name of Jesus for conceiving a child/children outside of wedlock.

Prayer Partner Speaks*

I witness the confession, repentance, and prayers of (your name) in regard to the practice of conceiving children outside of the boundaries of a committed, legal marriage. In the name of Jesus, I speak forgiveness to you for your and your family's named sins of conceiving children outside of wedlock. In the name of Jesus and through His precious shed blood, I release you from the curses of illegitimacy.

I command any and every spirit present to carry out these curses to leave (your name) right now in the name of Jesus. [Wait a moment for God to do this. Repeat this last command for each sin area renounced. Check with the Holy Spirit to be sure that any deliverance that was necessary has taken place.] I now speak healing, release and restoration from the effects of these curses.

For the case of you being the parent of illegitimate children: I and (your name) join together and command the curse of illegitimacy to come off (name of child/children's names).

Holy Spirit, I ask that you now come and comfort (your name) in these places of damage and pain. Lord would you please begin the process of restoration for every loss encountered from the damages inflicted.

*Please note that the Holy Spirit may bring up issues in this process that He wants to have uncovered—things that were, perhaps, not known. Listen and do what He says. Further, when commanding any spirits of curse to leave, watch to see what God is doing and give Him some time to bring about the cleansing) and release

Now, Holy Spirit, please come, cleanse, refill (your name) with Your presence in every place of damage, defilement,and curse. Please come and renew (your name's) mind in these areas where the curse of illegitimacy was a stronghold.

.

Chapter 9

The Ninth Doorway
It's Not What It Seems

You may be tempted to skip this chapter because idolatry doesn't seem to be in your background. But wait a minute and read on. You or your family may never, knowingly, have worshiped a false god or dabbled in witchcraft, horoscopes, crystals, fortune telling, or magic or participated in a non-Christian religion. But there are subtle disguises of idolatry and occultism that are behind these where you or your family may have unknowingly touched one of the forms of idolatry. Encountering something like one of the above will open a doorway to curse. Before we unpack the elements of this chapter, let's look at a couple examples, one affecting whole nations and one influencing a boy and his family. Then we can begin looking to see how some of the elements discussed in this chapter might give you a doorway to a better life.

The False Religion of Two Mass Murders

In the twentieth century, two men stand out as the biggest mass murderers of all time. Joseph Stalin, with the help of Vladimir Lenin, piled up a body count estimated by some sources to be twenty-three million while (Chairman) Mao Zedong has been attributed with up to seventy-eight million deaths. These individuals were not overthrown but died of natural causes; their statues and images still stand respected in the territories they once ruled. Many still mourn their passing. How can this be explained?

Most outside observers would attribute the slaughter and enslavement of the masses to despotic control, and indeed that was a major element. But surprisingly, in their two vast territories, the form of communism that was used to control the masses incorporated all the elements of a false religion (the practice of idolatry) with worship, adulation and pledges of loyalty.[5] Therefore, the millions upon millions who lived under their influences, those born later in these territories or to immigrants from there, are still under this spiritual control. Fresh flowers and adornments at the feet of many of their statues still venerate these despots. In China and the former USSR, the powerful effects of this form of false religion still permeates the thinking of the people, cultural norms, and continuing expectations of the government to supply their every need. Let's take a look at a less overarching, but nevertheless, powerful personal story illustrating how idolatry/occultism could find its way into the life of an individual.

Real Life Story

One of our new associate workers in the ministry in which we had a leadership position came to us for help with his son—we will call the boy Jens (not his real name). Jens had been an outstanding junior high student with top grades and good grooming, and he was well thought of by his teachers and fellow students. But now his grades had fallen badly, his appearance was poor, and he had withdrawn from most of his friends.

---

[5] Otto Bixler, *Widows, Orphans and Prisoners* (London, England, WC1E 6HJ: New Generation Publishing, 2009)

We met with Jens and his father to see what could be done. As we talked with Jens, we discovered that he was involved in a fantasy, role-playing game called Dungeons and Dragons. We explained how this game had an occult, idolatrous foundation that was not understood by them. As we carefully revealed the spiritual roots of the game, Jens renounced his involvement and confessed his unwitting sins. After some prayer, similar to that at the end of this chapter, he began to feel better, and the father noticed that the color of his son's eyes had changed from black to a beautiful blue (his former eye color). In the subsequent weeks, Jens' scholarship rebounded, and he was again full of life and socially interactive.

Idolatry, False Religions and Occultism

What a powerful section heading, stirring up all kinds of things in our imagination. But don't panic; the explanation is not that ominous or mysterious. Let's just take it one step at a time. Some of the things we're going to look at are quite commonplace in many lives, but the connection between them and our lack of well-being is quite unexpected. In the table on the next page, we categorize some contemporary, common sources of trouble. Then as the chapter unfolds, we will explain why these are doorways to a lack of well-being.

The key to this chapter is understanding the sin (and the law) of idolatry. The objective of this brief, conceptual study is to make us aware of deceptions that we and society in general may have been under. If we are going to escape from the power of idolatry, we must first see it. If we are to escape it and avoid it in the future, we must be able to recognize it in its many forms. When we don't see or recognize idolatry, we may fall prey to it. Let's now examine some basic concepts.

Some Sources of Idolatry and Occultism

Idolatry	Occultism
Non-Judeo-Christian Religions – False Gods	Horoscopes, Astrology, Crystals and New Age
Addictions and Substance Abuse, e.g., (see Chapter 6) Alcohol, Tobacco, Hallucinogens and Dissociative Drugs, Food Misuse	Witchcraft (white or otherwise), Satanism, evil eye, cursing and spells Ouija (Weeje) Board, Magic Eight Ball, Fortune-telling, Fantasy Role Playing Games (Dungeons and Dragons, etc.) and many Video Games using spells, magic powers, violence and killing, etc. Harry Potter, Pokémon (Japanese for pocket demon), etc.
Money & Position	Séances
Veneration of Persons – Chairman Mao, Stalin, Lenin, St. Peter, St Paul, St Mary, Buddha	Hypnotism, Superstitions Water Witching, Talismans

The first two of the *Ten Commandments,* Exodus 20:3-4, refer to idolatry. God is saying don't do it; it's not good for you. But idolatry seems to be, perhaps, the number one problem around the world. As Christians we may recognize that bowing down to or reverencing a statue (even of St Peter, Mary or Paul) or an image or false deity is idolatry, but we can also be drawn into some of the camouflaged, more subtle forms of idolatry. If we are deceived and lured into them, we ultimately come under their influence.

What Is Idolatry?

In a literal sense, worshiping a statue or image that represents a personality who lives (or lived) in the natural or spirit world (and asking that personality for help) is usually understood as idolatry. But idolatry can involve more than asking a false god (evil spirit) for your crops to grow, a wife for your son or for your health or business activity, etc. See Chapter 6 for a basic definition of idolatry.

Idolatry in its many forms can move stealthily into our lives because spirits of idolatry operate in cooperation with spirits of deception and mockery. And God wants us to come to Him rather than to these substitutes to supply all of our needs.

One of the reasons we can get caught up in idolatry is that we don't know what it is. Since idolatry can be deceiving, to be safe we need to ask, "What is idolatry?" It could be worshiping other gods, perhaps statues of stone, wood or metal, but this form of idolatry is quite obvious to most Christians. In Chapter 6 we examined some of the less obvious forms of idolatry. But first, let's look at the more simple, direct forms—ones that have named false deities and codified rituals of worship and service as well as their temples, regalia, etc. Our first guide to God's thoughts on idolatry is found in the *Ten Commandments*.

> *"You shall have no other gods before Me. You shall not make for yourself a carved image - any likeness of anything [or anyone], that is in heaven above, or that is in the earth beneath, or that is in the water under the earth*
>
> *Exodus 20: 3-4*

The Curses of Idolatry

Idolatry occupies the first two of the *Ten Commandments*. When we practice idolatry, we place ourselves under a curse, and this curse passes down our generation line to family members even to the fourth generation after us (Exodus 20:5). The results of idolatry's curses can take various forms in our lives. Let's take a look at some of the potential effects on us when we pass through the doorways of idolatry into disfavor.

Psalm 135 details some of the curses of idolatry that can come upon us and our family. These can also affect cities and nations.

> *The idols of the nations are but silver and gold, The work of man's hands.*
> *They have mouths, but they do not speak;*
> *They have eyes, but they do not see;*
> *They have ears, but they do not hear,*
> *Nor is there any breath at all in their mouths.*
> *Those who make them will be like them,*
> *Yes, everyone who trusts in them.*
> *Psalm 135: 15-18*

At first reading, these verses appear to be a description of the idols themselves. But verse 18 tells us that idolaters, those practicing idolatry, will display these same characteristics. Some of these marks of curse are obviously physical and some are more spiritual in effect. Let's take a look at both the physical and spiritual:

- We carry a long-term effect in our physical bodies.

- We also reap spiritual effects from the curse of idolatry.
- Speech difficulties, both in ordinary language expression and in the gift of tongues.
- Physical and spiritual sight can be diminished.
- Physical and spiritual hearing problems.
- Many breathing difficulties are associated with idolatry, including asthma, allergies, emphysema, lung cancer, etc.
- Psalm 115:7 tells us idolatry can also bring walking problems (i.e., foot, ankle, and leg) and problems with hands.
- Frequently, the physical problems affect areas that were involved with the idolatrous practice: knees that were bowed to idols; lips that kissed statues; fingers, hands, wrists and arms from rings, bracelets, and amulets worn; feet from which shoes were removed to visit a temple of false religion (even during sight-seeing).

The spiritual effects of idolatry beyond the physical could include:

- We read the Bible, but we don't really connect.
- We are sleepy in church or don't understand very well.
- Perhaps we are really having a hard time hearing God.
- Although we want to, we cannot speak in tongues.
- We do not seem to be able to exercise the spiritual gifts God has promised to believers.
- We want to be baptized in Holy Spirit, but somehow it doesn't happen when we are prayed for.

During prayer ministry, whether the person or someone in his/her family has been involved in idolatry, there may be noticeable reactions. As we begin to pray for healing, something of the spirit realm overcomes the afflicted and they may be unable to move, see, or hear as the spirits of idolatry, deception and mockery reveal themselves and their power. Once again, these spirits are allowed to exercise this power over an individual because of idolatrous sins and their attendant curses. All of these effects, both physical and spiritual, may be removed through prayer ministry.

Basic Steps to Eradicate Idolatry
Today in our personal past and in the recent generational past of our families (within four generations), there are many possible sources of organized idolatry, particularly from religion:

- Overt religions, for example: Buddhism, Hinduism Mormonism, Christian Science and other cults, Freemasonry,[6]
- Worshiping dead saints or séances, attempting to communicate with deceased friends or family
- Communism—with personal origins in a communist country, where we or our antecedents grew up (perhaps we did or didn't believe the party line), but if we cooperated in October Group, Pioneers, Komsomolsk, and the Party, then we or our family bowed down to the idols of Communism.

---

[6] Otto Bixler, *It Isn't Free And It Isn't Masonry* (Lancaster, England,LA2 0HN): Soverign World Ltd July 2, 2018)

Steps Toward Freedom from Idolatry and Its Curses

- First, we have to recognize the idolatry for what it is, or that it is there.
- Then we need to confess that we and/or our family were in idolatry.
- Then we must repent of the idolatrous practice(s). Next, we need to receive forgiveness from God, in the name of Jesus, through the prayer minister who is ministering to us.
- Then any spirits of idolatry, deception and mockery must be commanded to leave.

Our Personal Process to Deal with Idolatry

In the next section for prayer ministry release, we are dealing with the idolatry and false religions that you and your family practiced. There are several key elements involved in removing the influence of these practices from your life:

- Confession and repentance from your involvement by renouncing the practice or religion, its doctrines and each of the gods (idols) that were served.
- Commanding every evil spirit associated with the religion and its gods to leave you in Jesus' name.
- Removing all materials from the false religion/cult from your life and releasing you from ungodly soul ties (spiritual connections) to those in that religion/ occult practice.

Idolatry and Occultism: Stepping Through the Doorway to Freedom

The prayer ministry for this doorway covers both your direct and generational effects from idolatry. Again, we remind the reader that it is important to have a prayer partner during the ministry sessions. This partner is particularly helpful when releasing a person from the influence of evil spirits. Of course, you can pray through the issues in this chapter on your own, just you and God, but we have provided scripted prayers for both you and a prayer partner to facilitate and strengthen you in your passage from disfavor in life to favor. A typical prayer ministry for getting free from the idolatry of false religions and occultism is as follows:

Your Prayer and Declarations

Dear Heavenly Father, I come to You in Jesus name. I confess my sin (and those of my family) of being involved, believing, and practicing idolatry, a false religion of (name the religion cult) or idolatrous practice (e.g., communism, Christian Science, or other practices—see the table at the beginning of the chapter). I forgive my family members who practiced these things before me. I now repent and turn away from this false religion. I renounce all the doctrines and gods (idols). I now name (name the false gods or deities of this religion). I renounce any and all dedications and indoctrination ceremonies of (name each that you were involved with). I renounce all special names or identities received as a result of my involvement with (name the false religion). I ask that Your Holy Spirit would help me walk out of all of the practices and sins of this false religion.

Lord, I ask that You would forgive me for my sins of idolatry in (name the false religion /cult). Lord Jesus, I ask that You would now separate me from every individual with whom I have an ungodly soul tie/spiritual connection established in and through my involvement with (name the false religion/cult/ idolatrous practice). Please release me from the ungodly ties to (names of those who trained, indoctrinated, or led me or shared with me in this false religion or idolatrous practice).

Prayer Partner Speaks*

In the name of Jesus, I speak forgiveness to you for the sins of idolatry that you just confessed. In the name of Jesus, I command every spirit of idolatry, deception, false religion and mockery from (name the false religion/cult/idolatrous practice) to leave (name of the brother/sister) now. [Wait a moment for God to do this.] In the name of Jesus, I command the spirit of (name the god or idol renounced earlier) to leave (name of the brother/sister) now. [Wait a moment for God to do this. Repeat this last command for each god or idol renounced. Check with the Holy Spirit to be sure that all deliverance that was necessary has taken place.]

Lord, please separate (your name) from (his/her)

---

*Please note that the Holy Spirit may bring up issues in this process that He wants to have uncovered—things that were, perhaps, not known. Listen and do what He says. Further, when commanding any spirits of curse to leave, watch to see what God is doing and give Him some time to bring about the cleansing and release.

ungodly soul ties with (name of family members and names of other persons he/she was attached to in the false religion/idolatrous practice). Jesus, please return everything of (your name's) life to him/her that was wrongly invested in (names of family members and names of the persons with whom you were joined in the sin of idolatry) and release everything of this/ these persons from (your name). In the name of Jesus, I command every evil spirit that inhabited or influenced that relationship to now leave (your name).

Your Personal Actions Following Prayer Ministry

Everything (books, pamphlets, certificates, objects, images, pieces of jewelry, items of clothing, badges, emblems, trophies, awards, etc.) from the false religion, cult, idolatrous practice must be removed from your home, property, place where you work and be destroyed, not sold, or given away.

Chapter 10

The Tenth Doorway
Stepping on the Apple of God's Eye

A True Life Story

The United States Ambassador to the Court of Saint James's (Great Britain), 1938-1940, Joseph P. Kennedy, Sr. was a confirmed, vocal anti-Semitic. This man brought his opinions and beliefs to his job, influencing the leading nations of the world. Joseph's posturing against the Jews has not escaped worldwide notice.

In his book, *The Kennedy Curse,* Pulitzer Prize winning team journalist, Edward Klein, documents Joseph's opposition of the Jewish people and the subsequent effects upon the family.[7] Certainly, the Kennedys had other transgressions, but what we can take away from this authoritative, carefully crafted and researched secular documentary, is an impression of what may happen to a family standing against the Jewish people. In *The Kennedy Curse*, the author postulated that the Kennedys are indeed under a curse. The claim is backed up by a chronological list of untimely deaths in this wealthy and powerful man's family:

---

[7] Edward Klein, *The Kennedy Curse: Why Tragedy Has Haunted America's First Family for 150 Years* (New York: St. Martin's Press, 2004).

- Joseph P. Kennedy, Jr. – died in mysterious aircraft explosion in WWII, August 12, 1944.
- Kathleen Cavendish ("Kick") Kennedy – died in a plane crash over France, 1948.
- John F. Kennedy – President of the United States, assassinated on November 22, 1963.
- Robert F. Kennedy – assassinated in 1968.
- Edward Kennedy – drives off bridge killing passenger Mary Jo Kopechne, July 1969.
- David Kennedy – dies of an overdose of cocaine, April 25, 1984.
- Michael Kennedy (son of Robert F.) – an expert skier dies in ski accident, 1998.
- John F Kennedy, Jr. – dies in his crashed private plane, July 16, 1999.
- Edward Kennedy – dies an early death of brain cancer, 2009.
- Mary Kennedy, the estranged wife of Robert F. Kennedy Jr., committed suicide, May 16, 2012.
- Saoirse Kennedy Hill (granddaughter of Robert F.) died of drug overdose, 2019.
- Maeve Kennedy Townsend McKean and son Gideon McKean, descendants of Robert F. Kennedy, drown in a canoe accident, April 2, 2020.

Although *The Kennedy Curse* is a secular book, we can take a spiritual look at one of the contributing factors to the family curse. This hidden factor lies in God's plan for the Jewish people. Surprisingly, it deeply affects many the world over. Initially, it is hard to believe that such a thing has anything to do with our personal well-being; but wait a minute, in this chapter we are discovering a hidden doorway. If this curse was obvious to most, we wouldn't have included this here.

To help adjust our perspective, let's think about how celebrating Christmas and Easter spans the whole globe. Both holidays having their origins in ancient Jewish history have spilled over into the Christian and non-Christian worlds alike. Similarly, this hidden doorway has an effect that spans both time and distance to touch many lives.

Often overlooked in the Bible are two Scriptures revealing God's care and protectiveness of the Jewish people. These verses are so seldom read or understood we could almost believe they are hidden. They are often not emphasized or even spoken about in churches. The first verse, written by the minor prophet Zechariah nearly 2,500 years ago, tells us that if we unkindly treat those of Jewish ancestry, it is like we harshly touched (e.g., stepped on) the pupil of God's eye.

> *For thus says the LORD of hosts, "After glory He has sent me against the nations which plunder you, for he who touches you, touches the apple of His eye..."*
>
> *Zechariah 2:8*

You might wonder just what the consequences of such an action—touching the apple of God's eye—might be. The answer to this question is found in the first book of the Bible.

> *And I will bless those who bless you, and the one who curses you I will curse.*
>
> *Genesis 12:3*

In this second passage, God is speaking to Abraham, the father of the Jewish nation. So basically, anyone who blesses Israel (the descendants of Abraham) will be blessed. And conversely, those who would cause the Jews any amount of trouble, discomfort or embarrassment will suffer loss and trouble.

Anti-Semitism

What we are dealing with in the previous two verses today is called anti-Semitism. Perhaps you're thinking your attitude about Israel, whatever it might be, has no personal consequence. But read on to discover how you might be affected—if not by your personal behavior, then through your family, an organization, church, or country club, maybe even the citizenship in your nation. Let's take a look to see how these Scriptures work to reveal a hidden doorway.

But first we need to understand more about the word *curse*. It is used twice in Genesis 12:3, each time with a different meaning in the original Hebrew. The first time the word *curse* appears, it is explaining the act of someone cursing Israel. In this use, it is the Hebrew word, קָלַל *qalal*. According to Strong's Word 7043: קָלַל *qalal* refers to the attitude of a person who curses you. It incorporates the concepts of underlying contempt or despising, but it also incorporates the idea of treating lightly, lightly esteeming, superficially resisting, or trivializing.

When Genesis 12:3 talks about God cursing you in response, Strong's Word 779: אָרַר *'ārar* is used, a verb that denotes "to inflict with a curse." This verb, in a more specific sense, means "to bind (with a spell); to hem in with obstacles; to render powerless to resist." It is the same word for curse that is used in Genesis 3, where God says to the serpent, "Cursed are you more than all cattle, and more than every beast of the field" (Genesis 3:14 NAS), meaning that the serpent would be the lowest of all animals. This is the response of God toward the one who brings any level of trouble on the Jews in general or on one of Jewish ancestry.

108

So sensitive is God to the protection of those of Hebrew descent that He has proclaimed those who even lightly dishonor Jewish people will receive the same level of curse as the serpent in the Garden of Eden received.

An Ancient True Life Story

In the book of Esther, we can discover how God deals with hatred of the Jews. This historical recounting is a true life story about what happened to the man named Haman and his ten sons who tried to persecute and murder the Jews in ancient Susa. Haman, who was the king's highest ranking official, enacted legislation to kill all the Jews in King Ahasuerus' extended kingdom; but through the intercession of Queen Esther, the Jews were saved. However, Haman and his sons were all killed, Haman on the gallows and his sons by the sword. To this day, the Jews celebrate the feast of Purim in which they give thanks to God for delivering them from the plans of Haman.

A Contemporary Real-Life Story

Our friend, Ibolya Mezes, a medical doctor and pastor's wife in Budapest, Hungary, was asked to try to help a Christian woman who had been committed to a mental hospital. As in most Holy Spirit-led ministries, Ibolya was seeking to discover any spiritual causes/roots (doorways) for the woman's instability. As her time with the woman progressed, the roots of her affliction were discovered.

Although the woman was a Gentile, she had married a man of Jewish ancestry. It was in this marriage that the woman began to despise her husband and finally began to curse him as a Jew, saying that it would have been good if he had remained imprisoned in Auschwitz with his family where many Jews were murdered. It was only a short time later that she became so mentally unstable that it was necessary for her to be institutionalized.

We wish this woman's story had a happier ending, but she refused to repent of her hatred and condemnation of her husband and his Jewish ancestry. The last information we have is that she was still in the mental hospital. Confession, repentance, and forgiveness through the blood of Jesus are the necessary keys that would have led to her freedom and wholeness.

Anti-Semitism: A Hidden Root of Trouble in Our Lives

You may not have been directly involved in despising, hating, and persecuting the Jews. Yet, God's disfavor may be affecting your life through anti-Semitism. Let's look at a few ways that we may have been opened to this source of curse.

Sources of Anti-Semitism in Our Lives

- Our personal hatred, despising, persecution and withholding of favor toward persons of Jewish ancestry, including informing on Jews during times of persecution.

- Our direct bloodline predecessor's hatred, contempt, persecution, and withholding of favor toward persons of Jewish ancestry, including informing on Jews during times of persecution.
- Retelling jokes or demeaning stories about Jews.
- Being part of a group, family or organization that has been anti-Semitic. This includes nations that have not favored the Jews—certainly several Middle Eastern nations, but also Western nations that have stood against Israel and the Jews in general, or refused to help them directly, or opposed them in the United Nations.
- Some country clubs and other groups have had strict rules against having Jewish members.
- Some churches have subscribed to the heresy of "replacement theology" which teaches that God has rejected the Jews and Christians have replaced them in the eyes of His favor and future plans.

Anti-Semitism: Stepping Through the Doorway of Release

The first step in obtaining freedom from this curse is to recall or discover any places where you or anyone in your direct bloodline, or any group to which you or your family belong(ed) were involved in anti-Semitism. This process may involve praying for the Holy Spirit to remind you of your own involvement and asking your family about this practice in the family. Please remember that your nation may also have been involved with anti-Semitism.

The best practice in prayers of release is to have a "Prayer Partner" for this process, i.e., to ask at least one other

Christian to witness your repentance and speak forgiveness, healing, and release in the name of Jesus. Of course, you can pray through the issues in this chapter on your own, just you and God, but we have provided scripted prayers for both you and a prayer partner to facilitate your passage from disfavor in life to favor.

Your Prayer and Declarations

Dear Heavenly Father, I come to you in the precious name of Jesus. I confess and turn from my sins of anti-Semitism. (Tell Him what anti-Semitic things that you did, said, and/or believed in your heart.)

I also come to you with the anti-Semitic beliefs and practices of my family (church, group, organization I belonged to or nation I belonged to). I choose, by an act of my will, to forgive (name the persons, group, etc.) for (name the things done or believed) which opened the doors of curse into my life. I renounce these beliefs and practices in the name of Jesus.

Heavenly Father, I also renounce and repent of the anti-Semitic practices of my nation and all instances where it resisted, persecuted or did not support Israel or the Jews in general.

Lord, I now ask you to forgive me in the name of Jesus for these sins of anti-Semitism. I claim the shed blood of Jesus over these sins.

Prayer Partner Speaks*

I witness the confession, repentance, and prayers of (your name) in regard to anti-Semitism. In the name of

Jesus, I speak forgiveness to you, for your and your family's (nation, church, organization, etc). named sins of anti-Semitism. In the name of Jesus and through His precious shed blood, I release you from the curses of anti-Semitism. I command any and every spirit present to carry out these curses to leave (your name) right now in the name of Jesus. I now speak healing, release and restoration from the effects of these curses.

Now, Holy Spirit, please come to cleanse and refill (your name) with Your presence in every place of damage and defilement. Please come and renew (your name's) mind in these areas where anti-Semitism was a stronghold.

*Please note that the Holy Spirit may bring up issues in this process that He wants to have uncovered—things that were not known. Listen and do what He says. Further, when commanding any spirits of curse to leave, watch to see what God is doing and give Him some time to bring about the cleansing and release.

Chapter 11

The Eleventh Doorway
Whose Was It?

Yours or Someone Else's?

Taking something that doesn't belong to you may be an issue that has touched your life. It has kept many in the land of adversity. Our real-life example for the *Eleventh Doorway* originated in Yerevan, Armenia, in full view of Mt. Ararat where Noah's ark touched down after the flood.

Real-Life Story

My mind was racing as I organized my thoughts before addressing a recently freed, post-communist group of people. They had gathered to hear a message about the love of God and His healing powers for the afflicted. Many were already in the meeting hall when a man with intense back pain came up to me requesting healing prayer. It was not a good time to disrupt my preparation for the message to the whole group. I wanted to help, but thought, "Maybe God will bring relief to him, as He often does in our meetings." I told him that if he didn't get relief as I was bringing the message, I would see him afterward when my mind was clear.

After the meeting, the man came to me again, saying that his back pain was still there. Now I was more relaxed, and silently I asked God for the key to the man's affliction. Suddenly this word appeared in my

115

mind: "stolen." Of course, I didn't know the significance of the word yet, so I began asking him a few questions to discover how to help him.

"Do you know Jesus as your Savior?" I asked. "Yes," he answered. "Show me where your back pain is located," I requested. Whereupon he pointed to the lower part of his back. Then I asked him, "Just how long have you had this back pain?" He said, "About twelve years." I commented, "That's a long time of suffering." And he agreed.

So, then I asked, "Do you remember how the pain began?" "Yes," he said. "I leaned over to pick up a small metal can of gasoline and the pain came." Using my one piece of information [*stolen*] from God, I inquired, "Oh, was that can of gasoline yours?" "His face turned white, and he said, "No, I was stealing it! I had not given my life to Jesus yet and did not understand it to be wrong. While under communism, times were difficult and survival was paramount."

Twelve years ago, unknowingly, he had crossed over God's boundaries from the land of blessings to the land of adversity. The way back was simple. Immediately he realized he was living in the land of adversity and needed to go through what we are now calling the *Eleventh Doorway* to escape his symptoms. He prayed with me a simple confession and repentance prayer for his sin of stealing, something similar to the escape prayers from our first ten chapters. I spoke forgiveness to him and began to speak healing to him, all in the name of Jesus.

116

We were both surprised as the pain immediately jumped to his shoulder and then to other parts of his body. It was a spirit of infirmity that came upon him that day twelve years earlier as he stepped into the land of adversity. It was then necessary to command this afflicting spirit to go from him as he had now stepped through the doorway of escape and into the land of blessings. As I did that, he was instantly healed of the back pain!

Stealing

Stealing can take many forms and, in some cases, it will also involve lying, the subject of our next chapter. Maybe some of these sins have touched your or your family's life:

Employees take home office supplies, pens, paper, scotch tape, paper clips, thumbtacks, erasers, pencils, envelopes, postal stamps and more. Sometimes workplace tools are taken: wrenches, files, hammers, oil, grease, cosmetics. In the food industry, meat, cheese, sugar and flour are taken home; or foods, even whole meals, that were never paid for are consumed in the workplace.

The list goes on and on for things people take from their place of employment. Many justify it by saying, "They don't pay me enough," "I need it," "They are not nice to me," or "They have lots of money and will never miss it." Some steal money from their employer; others take finished goods. Some steal time by not working efficiently, or by various ruses, including finding ways to sleep on the job, using the internet for their own purposes on company time, and making personal phone calls while they are on the job.

Some turn in false reports of their expenses when serving off-site and get reimbursed for expenses they never incurred, or they use company equipment or vehicles for their own purposes.

The problem is, when we do these things, like the man from Armenia, we cross over to the land of adversity. Back pain is not the only trouble we may have invited on ourselves. Let's take a look at the doorway relating to stealing that stands between the lands of adversity and blessings.

What the Bible Says about Stealing

Taking things that do not belong to us is forbidden by God. The first place where we see a declaration of this is in the *Ten Commandments*.

You shall not steal.

Exodus 20:15,
Deuteronomy 5:19

There are numerous Scripture portions that deal with stealing and some with the resultant effect on the thief and his family/household. Whenever we go against the will of God, we will find ourselves outside of His favor, and often we find adversity facing us. When a thief was discovered, not only was there the loss of social favor, but the thief was required to repay that which he had stolen with a penalty.

But when he is found (out) he must repay sevenfold. He must give all the substance of his house.

Proverbs 6:30

118

Theft often takes place under the cover of darkness, but if somehow the sun comes up and the thief is discovered, there is a penalty for his misdeeds.

> *He shall make restitution; if he owns nothing, then he shall be sold [into slavery] for his theft.*
>
> *Exodus 22:3*

> *If [he has stolen livestock and] what he stole is actually found alive in his possession ... he shall pay double [their value].*
>
> *Exodus 22:4*

In 1 Corinthians we are informed that thieves will not be received into heaven.

> *... nor thieves ... will inherit the kingdom of God.*
> *1 Corinthians 6:10*

Stealing: Stepping Through the Doorway of Release

The first step in obtaining freedom from this curse is to recall or discover any places where you or anyone in your direct bloodline, or any group or gang to which you or your family belong(ed), were involved with stealing. This process may involve praying for the Holy Spirit to remind you of your stealing. You may also need to ask your family about stealing in the family. Please remember that your nation or a group you belong(ed) to may not have a righteous history. Nations steal territory; governments confiscate property; people groups are known for their thievery.

119

The best practice in prayers of release is to have a "Prayer Partner" stand with you for this process, i.e., have at least one other Christian witness your repentance and speak forgiveness, healing and release to you in the name of Jesus. Of course, you can pray through the issues in this chapter on your own, just you and God, but we have provided scripted prayers for both you and a prayer partner to facilitate your passage from disfavor in life to favor.

Your Prayer and Declarations

Dear Heavenly Father, I come to you in the precious name of Jesus. I confess and turn from my sins of stealing and thievery (name all specific instances that you can recall).

I also come to you with these same sins that have been in my family (and/or nation/people group to which I belong[ed]). I choose, by an act of my will, to forgive (name the persons or groups) for stealing by which they opened the doors of curse into my life. I renounce these practices in the name of Jesus. I give you any anger, bitterness, hatred and judgments against those who opened these doorways into my life.

Heavenly Father, I agree to not continue to benefit from the things taken from others that did not belong to me. I also pledge to return what has been taken or to compensate those who have suffered loss from my stealing/thievery. Please show me the way to carry out compensation where possible.

Lord, I now ask you to forgive me in the name of Jesus for these sins of thievery/stealing. I claim the shed blood of Jesus over these sins.

Prayer Partner Speaks*

I witness the confession, repentance, and prayers of (your name) in regard to thievery/stealing. In the name of Jesus, I speak forgiveness to you for your and your family's named sins of stealing/thievery.

In the name of Jesus and through His precious shed blood, I release you from the curses associated with thievery/stealing. I command any and every spirit present to carry out these curses, to leave (your name) right now in the name of Jesus. [Wait a moment for God to do this. Repeat this last command for each sin area renounced. Check with the Holy Spirit to be sure that any necessary deliverance has taken place.] I now speak healing, release and restoration from the effects of these curses.

Now, Holy Spirit, please come and cleanse and refill (your name) with Your presence in every place of damage and defilement through these practices. Please come and renew (your name's) mind in these areas where thievery/stealing was a stronghold.

Holy Spirit, I ask that you now come and assist (your name) in the process of repayment/compensation and restitution to those whom he/she victimized through theft where it is possible to do so.

*Please note that the Holy Spirit may bring up issues in this process that He wants to have uncovered—things that were, perhaps, not known. Listen and do what He says. Further, when commanding any spirits of curse to leave, watch to see what God is doing and give Him some time to bring about the cleansing and release from the sins of thievery/stealing.

Chapter 12

The Twelfth Doorway
The Absolute Truth

Truth and the Opposite

In this chapter we will examine God's wishes for us to be truth tellers, not liars. In the following story, a man tried to tell a real whopper, to mislead a conference hall full of God seekers. But in everyday life, there are many times when we can step through the doorway to adversity by not telling the *absolute truth*.

A Real-Life Story

> The Iron Curtain had just fallen. Over 1,000 post-communist delegates funneled through the registration area and into the meeting hall of the former Communist Trade Workers Union in Budapest, Hungary. All excitedly anticipated several days of receiving concentrated doses of God's truths and healing transformation—something denied them in the former USSR. Amid the cacophony of Hungarian, Russian, Romanian, Polish and Ukrainian voices filling the registration gallery, God spoke to me saying, "Do you see that man over there? I don't want him in My conference." In his long, black priestly robes, he would have been hard to miss, but I couldn't get to him before one of my conference staffers had registered him complete with an entrance badge. Oh no! My worker, my disobedience!

I grabbed my best friend, a former soviet (KGB) hotel security guard and rushed over to the man in the priestly robes before he could get into the conference hall. "Hi," I said. "What brought you to this conference?" "I have a message for the people," he responded. I replied, "Interesting, just what is it?" He quickly came back saying, "I cannot tell you."

Confronting him I said, "Sorry, you're going to have to tell me. I am the conference organizer, and nothing happens in there without my permission." We went around and around, me insisting and him refusing. In the middle of the confrontation, God told me everything about the man's secret message, so I switched tactics.

"Okay, if you won't tell me what it is, then I will tell you. You are from Moldavia and your secret message for the people is that New Jerusalem is under your country." He gasped and said, "Yes, how did you know that!?" "Listen," I said, "It is not under your country; the Bible tells us the size of New Jerusalem is 1500 miles by 1500 miles by 1500 miles and your country is much smaller than that. Further, the Bible says that New Jerusalem comes down from heaven, not up from under the earth. You are a liar and a fraud!" I snatched his registration badge off his chest and had him thrown out of the building!

Amazing! When God asks us to do something, even what seems impossible, He is right there if we are obedient, He will assist us to carry out His wishes. God is truthful and His truth is bigger than any lie. He wants only the absolute truth for you and me. In this instance, God was exposing a lie about to be propagated in order to protect over 1,000 people who were wanting to hear about Him and His truths, not to hear religious lies.

Now let's take a look at the life of a man attending a local church who decided to use untruth as a means to take care of himself.

Another Real-Life Story

In Budapest, Hungary, we pastored a church with about thirty percent Africans who left their countries in desperation, coming north to find a better life. These Africans were refugees in every sense of the word, most in dire circumstances with seemingly no way to support themselves. Our congregation also gave physical food to a number of them as we brought the truth of God into their lives.

Big Billy, a Nigerian refugee, not yet *born-again*, was one who began attending our Sunday services for networking and support. But for many months I did not see him in church; I had heard he was in prison. And then one Sunday morning there he was. "Pastor Otto," he asked, "would you please pray for me?" "Oh, hi, Billy. What's up?" I replied. He said, "My girlfriend left me while I was in prison and cleaned out everything I had in my apartment. I have nothing!" "I'm sorry to hear that," I said, "but I did see you drive up in your Mercedes this morning?" "She couldn't sell it because it has a fake registration and license plates," he replied.

"So just what do you want me to pray for, Billy?" I
asked. "For my *business*; I just need to make one more
good deal to get out of the hole I am in." "Billy," I
replied, "I know what your business is; it got you sent
to prison for deceiving people and taking their money
for things that you never intended to deliver. I am so
sorry, Billy; you know that God will not receive a
prayer for your deceptive business. But let me pray for
you, for God's honest provision, and for bringing your
life into His ways that He might rescue you from all
the painful adversity you are suffering under."

Note: Billy was not yet convicted of his sin, nor was he repentant.
He had not yet made the connection between his going to prison
and the lying, deception, and taking people's money without
giving them something of value in return.

Perhaps you wouldn't consider yourself a liar like Billy, or
the false priest in Budapest, but think about how you
handle the truth. If a government agent were to carefully
examine your yearly tax forms, would they find that you
had misrepresented your net income to avoid paying more
taxes? Mistakes are one thing, but deliberately falsifying
your income is a lie.

Taking credit for something good that you didn't do is a
lie. Blaming someone else for something you did wrong is
a *lie*. Claiming ignorance when you knew full well what the
situation was is a *lie*. The list is endless for covering up the
truth. Selling your property without disclosing hidden
defects is lying, as is hiding mistakes you have made in
your workplace while employed. Perhaps you cheated in
school examinations or plagiarized an essay or term paper.

We have been created to be truth tellers. But without trusting in God to take care of us, we often wind up trying to take care of ourselves by misrepresenting the truth in order to get something we want, to hurt someone we are angry at, or to avoid the consequences of our wrongdoing, mistakes, or poor performance.

Your Choice—Truth or Lies
God's Ways or Satan's Ways

So, how does God feel about the truth? What are His standards for truth and how can we meet them? To begin with, let's look at some of the names that God has chosen for Himself to represent His character. As His children, these characteristics are what He wishes us to exemplify on earth.

In all things, God is a Truth-Teller. Before we go further, let's look at the Apostle Paul's letter to Titus, now canonized into the Bible as the Book of Titus. In the second verse of this epistle, Paul speaks of "… *God, who cannot lie* …" So, we see here that God doesn't lie but exemplifies the truth. And He wants us to emulate His truthfulness. Whenever we are not truthful, we step through a spiritual doorway that separates us from God and His ways to enter the land of adversity.

Often as we pursue our own desires and wishes, we are led to "bend the truth," misleading others to get what we think we want. But in so doing, we have made an unwitting choice to identify ourselves with untruth, i.e., lies. And when we identify with lies, guess who we are emulating: the devil! And by emulating the devil, we can ultimately

127

find ourselves in opposition to God and His ways. But we have a choice: we can emulate God and receive blessings, or we can copy the devil and receive curses. Jesus, while addressing a group of individuals persecuting Him, informed them whom they were following.

> *You are of your father the devil, and you want to do the desires of your father. He was a murderer from the beginning and does not stand in the truth because there is no truth in him. Whenever he speaks a lie, he speaks from his own nature, for he is a liar and the father of lies.*
>
> *John 8:44*

When we lie and deceive, we are emulating the devil, aligning ourselves with his untruth.

The Gold Standard—God and His Truth

Two parts of God's personality or being, Jesus and the Holy Spirit, are named Truth. The first place we can see Jesus called "the truth" is in the Book of John.

> *Jesus said to him, "I am the way, and the truth, and the life; no one comes to the Father but through Me."*
>
> *John 14:5*

Further on in John 14:17 Jesus promised, following His return to heaven, to send the Holy Spirit to believers. Here He called the Holy Spirit the "Spirit of truth."

> *I will ask the Father, and He will give you another Helper, that He may be with you forever; that is the Spirit of truth, whom the world cannot receive,*

128

because it does not see Him or know Him, but you know Him because He abides with you and will be in you.

John 14:16,17

Continuing in the Book of John, we also discover that God the Father is identified with *truth*.

When the Helper comes, whom I will send to you from the Father, that is the Spirit of truth who proceeds from the Father, He will testify about Me,

John 14:26

While we first saw that Jesus and the Holy Spirit are being directly named as representing *truth*, we now discover that the Father Himself is also the source of *truth*. The whole of God represents *truth*. Therefore we, who are made in God's image, can choose to walk in God's truthful ways, even when formerly we were walking in untruth. All we have to do is decide and act. Ask today for help from the Holy Spirit, the *Helper,* to enable you to walk out of your ways and the world's ways of lies and deception.

But when He, the Spirit of truth, comes, He will guide you into all the truth.

John 14:13

Choosing Restoration

If we traffic in lies and deception in direct opposition to God's ways, we will pass through a doorway to adversity in this life. And we also will not find ourselves in heaven at the end of our life—a truly personal tragedy which can be averted.

He who overcomes will inherit these things, and I will be his God and he will be My son. But for the cowardly and unbelieving, and abominable, and murderers, and sexually immoral persons, and sorcerers, and idolaters, and all liars, their part will be in the lake that burns with fire and brimstone, which is the second death.

Revelation 21:7, 8

So, let us see how to escape from the land of destruction through the doorway to restoration. Please pray through the following prayer ministry section.

Lies and Deception: Stepping Through the Doorway of Release

The first step in obtaining freedom (restoration) from the destruction brought on by lies and deception is to recall or discover any places where you or anyone in your direct bloodline, or any group to which you or your family belong(ed) were involved with these sins.

This process may involve praying for the Holy Spirit to convict your heart of any places in your life, currently or in the past, where you were involved in these sins. You may also need to ask your family about lying and deception in the family. Please remember that your nation or a group you belong(ed) to may not have a righteous history. Nations lie and deceive other countries; governments deceive their citizens; people groups are known for their deception.

The best practice in prayers of release is to have a "Prayer Partner" stand with you for this process, i.e., to have at

130

least one other Christian witness your repentance and speak forgiveness, healing and release to you in the name of Jesus. Of course, you can pray through the issues in this chapter on your own, just you and God, but we have provided scripted prayers for both you and a prayer partner to facilitate your passage from disfavor in life to favor.

Your Prayer and Declarations

Dear Heavenly Father, I come to you in the precious name of Jesus. I confess and turn from my sins of lying to and deceiving (name all specific instances that you can recall).

I also come to you with these same sins that have been in my family (name any family members and their instances of lying and deceiving that you are aware of as well as those of your nation/ people group to which you belong[ed]) and repent for their sins of lying and deception. I choose, by an act of my will, to forgive (name the persons I was associated with or groups) for lying to others and deceiving them, by which doors of curse were opened into my life. I renounce these practices in the name of Jesus. I give you any anger, bitterness, hatred, and judgments against those who opened these doorways into my life.

Heavenly Father, I agree to not continue to benefit from the things obtained from others that I did not deserve, which were obtained through lies and deceit. Please show me any way you wish me to step away from benefits received through my use of untruth and the avoidance of truth.

Lord, I now ask you to forgive me in the name of Jesus for these sins of lying and deception. I claim the shed blood of Jesus over these sins.

Prayer Partner Speaks*

I witness the confession, repentance, and prayers of (your name) in regard to lying and deception. In the name of Jesus, I speak forgiveness to you for your and your family's named sins of lying and deception. In the name of Jesus and through His precious shed blood, I release you from the curses associated with lying and deception. I command any and every spirit present to carry out these curses to leave (your name) right now in the name of Jesus. [Wait a moment for God to do this. Repeat this last command for each sin area renounced. Check with the Holy Spirit to be sure that any necessary deliverance has taken place.] I now speak healing, release and restoration from the effects of these curses.

Now, Holy Spirit, please come and cleanse and refill (your name) with Your presence in every place of damage and defilement through these practices. Please come and renew (your name's) mind in these areas where lying and deception was a stronghold.

Holy Spirit, I ask that you come and assist (your name) in the process of bringing the truth in place of lies and deception where it is Your wish and it would be fruitful to do so.

*Please note that the Holy Spirit may bring up issues in this process that He wants to have uncovered—things that were, perhaps, not known. Listen and do what He says. Further, when commanding any spirits of curse to leave, watch to see what God is doing and give Him some time to bring about the cleansing and release.

Epilogue

For many of you, discovering the *Twelve Ancient Doorways to Freedom* has already been life changing: We're so excited for you and what God has done; that's just what we hoped for! For others, while it has been an eye-opener and you've begun the journey to a better life, somehow it seems there's a way to go in passing through one or more of the ancient doorways. Going through an ancient doorway is a process or journey and both conditions above are normal. If your passage seems not complete, don't be discouraged. Every individual is on his/her own journey with differing life experiences, starting points, past damages, giftings, and the destiny God has for you. As you have been faithful to enter the journey with God, He will complete that which He has drawn you into doing. Passage is the beginning of a process of renewal to be worked out in your continuing life.

> *For I am confident of this very thing, that He who began a good work in you will perfect it until the day of Christ Jesus.*
>
> *Philippians 1:6*

Fulfilling the Book's Promises

In the Epilogue we are addressing the question of going further or completing the promised passage to freedom through one or more of the ancient doorways when, personally, something seems not quite finished. Relax a little, thank God for what He has begun in you, give Him

133

all your doubts and fears, and get ready to partner with Him in the continuing journey of your life.

Take a moment right now and acknowledge these things in prayer. You are better off than you were when you started your journey through the *Twelve Ancient Doorways to Freedom*. For us all it is, however, a journey. Now your eyes are opened, and you are more spiritually aware of yourself and the effects of being out of God's order. You are so much better off than those who have yet to make the same discoveries that you have made. Now let's look at the *process of passage* and some possible hindrances that can be removed.

The Way Forward

The way forward is attainable to anyone who has decided to continue with God; and while conceptually quite simple, it may take some determination, time, and effort—but it is worth it. Let's review some of the things that will make your forward progress possible. Some of these are obvious, some are not, and some may be obscured by what we thought or believed about God and His ways. A few possible hindrances to your progress are addressed in the Appendix and will be looked at in outline form at the end of the Epilogue. But first let's see how some past life experiences and personal practices could be holding you back from the freedom that God promises.

Walking Out of Past Practices

There's a spiritual process intrinsic to this book:

- After reading the true contemporary stories of others who received miraculous blessings from

God, our faith rises, facilitating our belief that God could and would help us in similar ways.

- Getting a Biblical understanding of the process necessary to pass through God's hidden-in-plain-sight ancient doorways to freedom, i.e., to walk out of the difficulties that our and our family's transgressions had brought into our life.
- Discovering twelve common potential areas of affliction and the doorways to escape.
- Learning the simple, biblically-legal scripted prayer sequences (forms of confession, repentance and forgiveness) which aid in stepping through the spiritual doorways of your afflictions to freedom.

Overcoming Habitual Practices

For some of you, after praying the prayers of escape as outlined in this book, the matter is over and your freedom from the afflictions of transgression will either begin suddenly or gradually, depending upon the circumstances. However, for others of us, there are habits to overcome. Our lifestyle or life patterns may incorporate habitual sinful practices that, once in place, became intrinsic to our behavior/personality, i.e., lying, stealing, overeating, sexual immorality, or judging others, to name a few.

The next steps for those with habitual sin involves a continuing discipleship under the influence of the Holy Spirit. We may find that we are still entering the same wrong behavior patterns which we have just been convicted of, repented from, and renounced. The problem is not that we are a bad person or beyond the reach of God's helping hand. Often it is a matter of changing our life practices.

However, we may find this is not so easy, and many become aware that the desired change is beyond our unassisted self. We are going to have to call upon God to help us and be ruthless in battling these destructive and self-harming practices.

In overcoming habitual practices, we need to take advantage of God's availability as a Helper, something that maybe no one ever told you about. Conceptually, this is different from just crying out to God for favor; it is entering into a cooperative partnership with Him.

> *I will ask the Father, and He will give you another Helper, that He may be with you forever; that is the Spirit of truth, whom the world cannot receive, because it does not see Him or know Him, but you know Him because He abides with you and will be in you."*
>
> *John 14:16,17*

As in any partnership, there will be duties, responsibilities, and functions that each party will carry out. In beginning this cooperative relationship, we need to be honest with God about our struggles, telling Him that we intend to stop our wrongdoing pattern. Then we need to humble ourselves and ask Him for help (for Him to manifest Himself in His promised role as a Helper). Amazingly, you can enter into a two-way agreement with God when you enlist His help. For example, you could ask Him (as His part) to intervene in your life, to warn you when you are in circumstances where you might fail in your battle against habitual sin. Your part of the agreement would be to take heed of His warnings and, to the best of your abilities, avoid a sinful response in the circumstances where you would have previously acted in an ungodly way. Ask Him to bring to your attention the choices you have in a testing circumstance before you fail. Let's look at a real-life example of how this might work.

Back in the 1980's we were leading a discipleship group for those trying to stop overeating, i.e., to eat healthy. For some of the group, it was a real battle, one they were not winning. Finally, we led the group into a prayer of commitment, asking God to help each of them in shopping for and bringing home healthy food from the supermarket. At our next discipleship meeting, one particularly overweight member gave the following testimony:

"As I was walking along the supermarket aisle, I began to reach for some unhealthy comfort food and the still, quiet, loving voice of the Lord said, "No, don't buy that." But His voice was so gentle and quiet that I easily ignored it in my habitual self-comforting cycle. I didn't heed His instruction. I continued to reach out, grabbing the item. I was shocked as He next shouted into my ear, "Stop!" My response to Him was, "Ok, Ok! You didn't have to shout!" But truthfully, He needed to shout as I was subconsciously following my old habits of buying my favorite, unhealthy comfort food."

If God would speak so clearly to someone struggling with an issue as simple as getting his/her diet right, how much more would He speak to us in our afflictions? Ask Him for help and expect that He will be there by your side. He is who He says He is and a rewarder of those who seek Him.

... he who comes to God must believe that He is and that He is a rewarder of those who seek Him.
Hebrews 11:6

If food, alcohol, drugs, cigarettes, chocolate (sweets) have been something that troubled you, they need to be removed from your home, car, office drawer, etc. Maybe you will need to avoid pathways that go past the tobacco shop, the ice cream shop, sweet shop, bakery, or liquor store. There may be aisles in the supermarket that you need to avoid. Those of us dealing with substance abuse/addictions must not hide a secret stash of liquor, chocolate, tobacco, or drugs somewhere just in case there is an emergency need. You won't have that need if you start depending on God.

If you were having a problem with pornography and/or masturbation, remove all literature, photos, etc., that were supporting these practices from your life, home, office, car, and websites from your computer/smartphone. We must be ruthless in standing against our past bad habits. We will need to stop social involvement with those who support our wrong habits and perhaps avoid restaurants, pubs, bars and newsstands or magazine racks where temptation resides.

What Happens When I Fail?

Establishing a new habit is just the same as learning to walk, swim, ride a bicycle, or walk on a tightrope. Failure is part of the process and to expect otherwise is unrealistic. God is our safety net. Quitting the fight for freedom is not an option if we wish for the benefits. Each of our mistakes is a learning platform from which to launch our next attack on attaining new levels of freedom and holiness. So, what can we do when we fall back into our old ways?

The first step is to stand against the guilt and accusations of the enemy: This is just a learning process. Go immediately to God in prayer and tell Him you're sorry and ask Him to help you understand what happened and to coach you for success. Ask Him to help you be more aware of circumstances next time and to hear His voice amid your retraining battle. Your old habits are not impossible to escape, but it may be a process.

Of course, food, substance abuse, pornography, or masturbation may not be your problem, so what about other afflictions that need to be escaped? Our battles and the necessary partnership with God to change our behavior will be similar. Read on to see some other examples. Ultimately, we are just helping you discover God's help and, in the space of a short book like this one, we cannot address every problem. But rest assured, He can and will help you with your specific problem if you give Him the chance.

Dealing with Roots and Fruits

Sometimes the very problem we are focusing on and trying to deal with is not the primary issue, even though it is indeed a sin that brings trouble in our life; it may be the fruit of an underlying root problem. With bad fruit, we can keep on attacking, and dealing with the presenting specific sin fruit of our life without getting complete victory. But it just may be that we need to take an axe to the root (cause). It does not excuse our presenting sin symptoms, but maybe it is there from a yet-to-be discovered causal problem that keeps on producing bad fruit: a yet-to-be remembered past hurt, damage, trauma, or long-term life situation. Our response to these forgotten circumstances could have resulted in the establishment (the putting in place) of a sinful coping mechanism that is now operated by our subconscious mind. Not every difficulty in walking through the hidden, ancient doorways to freedom will be established in a forgotten incident or circumstance, but some will.

In Chapters 4 and 5, we met Sarah who had to work through some very difficult *father issues* resulting from long-term abuse in her childhood. In Chapter 5 we discovered that in her adolescence she had finally been able to confront her father about her abuse. In her now more adult body and maturing understanding, in anger she was able to stop the abuse by telling her father that she was no longer going to be a victim.

The problem was in her yet-to-become-an-adult understanding; she made a mistake. Believing her anger to be the power that delivered her from abuse (rather than her father's fear of exposure as an abuser), she began to experiment in using anger in other situations where she felt threatened and became something of an abuser herself. The sinful fruit she discovered was taking control of situations by using anger. But the root cause was the mistaken belief that anger was her powerful deliverer.

This belief came from the past traumatic confrontation of her father. For her, she had to step into the arms of Jesus as her protector and renounce (lay an axe to the root of) self-sufficiency (manifested as self-protection). While the

140

presenting symptom (fruit) was verbally abusing others in anger, the root was her fear of being victimized again and using anger to protect her in perceived danger. This was the sin of self-sufficiency.

Let's look at a few possible situations where sinful fruit is not standing alone but is supported by a hidden or at least not-so-obvious root. Perhaps one of the following is similar to a root keeping you from passing through one of God's ancient doorways to freedom.

Possible Fruits and Roots

Fruits	Roots
Lies, bragging, pride	Childhood rejection Lack of affirmation
Stealing	Poverty and deprivation
Temper problems	Previous victimization Family tempers
Self-sufficiency	Lack of nurture, provision, deprivation
Unforgiveness	Unresolved childhood trauma
Judgmentalism	Childhood rejection

Helpful Hints

Meeting the following criteria will increase your ability to pass through God's ancient doorways to freedom.

- **Decision**

  You need to decide to go forward and tell God that you have decided to go through the doorway to freedom, asking for His help to do so.

- **Salvation**

  Going forward requires that you are a Christian, having received Jesus Christ as your personal Savior. Salvation is not a result of attending church, although it is helpful. Please be careful here. It is not just a beginning assent to the concept of God being real, but a heart conviction, a commitment to Jesus, and a declaration before others of your belief and dedication. Please go through the *Appendix*, reading the "Introduction" and "Salvation" sections, making sure that you pray the Salvation Prayer.

- **Lordship**

  The reader must understand that belonging to God's family is not just an internal conviction; it will result in changes in your behavior brought about by God acting in your life. But we need to give Him permission to bring about changes in our behavior and thought life. Continue in the *Appendix* and work through the section on "Lordship." Be sure to pray the prayer of personal dedication in the box titled "Lordship Prayer."

- **Entering God's Family Behavior**

  Once we have received Jesus as our Savior and made Him Lord over our whole life, there should begin to be some evidence of change in our life that results in our starting to look more like a member of God's family in word and deed. Work through the rest of the *Appendix*: the section on "The Next Steps." Amazingly, God wants to transform your life and empower you to be one of His people of action here on earth.

- **Becoming Born-again**

Many have believed that if you have received Jesus as your Savior, you are "born-again." This belief is a partial truth and is a barrior of misunderstanding which has resulted in believers being powerless! Becoming "born-again" is a process (God's further workmanship in the believer) which first includes believing in Jesus as Savior. The rest of the process enables ordinary believers to hear the voice of God and enables them to perform the good works that He promises we will do. Without this further processing, we cannot do His promised "good works," or be what He intended for us to be here on earth.

For we are His workmanship, created in Christ Jesus for good works, which God prepared beforehand so that we would walk in them.
                                        Ephesians 2:10

We need to get past this barrier of misunderstanding, truly become "born-again" to enter the exciting world of hearing God and doing His works. Now work your way through the next *Appendix* section, "The Two Baptisms." Once you have studied this section, then be sure that you obtain both baptisms to become truly born-again.

- **Cleansing of Our Soul**

  There are a number of things that can hold us back, both from passing through some of God's doorways to freedom and from being empowered through the baptism of the Holy Spirit. Both goals are related to being dependent on holiness and freedom from other spiritual claims on our life. Work through the last section of the *Appendix*, "Blockages to Holy Spirit Baptism." Having studied this section, work through removing any personal blockages that you discovered there. Ask God to reveal any other hidden blockages of which you were unaware and then prayerfully remove those. Your prayers for removal of hidden blockages can be modeled after the prayers found at the ends of the chapters in this book.

APPENDIX

Salvation and Lordship

Introduction

Twelve Ancient Doorways to Freedom is an eye-opening book for most. It shows ordinary people the way of escape from a dozen common trouble areas in our lives to attain relief and the blessings of God. Even typical churchgoers rarely have the training, understanding, and spiritual strength to escape these hidden spiritual traps by themselves.

In the introduction at the beginning of the book, we mentioned that one of the spiritual requirements for passage through to the doorways of escape is your belonging to God. Anyone can avoid the "dirty dozen" spiritual pitfalls of life documented in this book once their eyes have been opened to them. But to escape, once having fallen into them, is another matter. Let's first take a look at the idea of belonging to God wherein He provides you with everything you'll need to get all the benefits we've written about in this book. Perhaps a simple story will help in understanding what it means to belong to God.

Marley's Story

Some years ago, our family decided to get a dog. Going to the city animal shelter, we found a beautiful black lab mix dog that had been previously taken from and returned to the shelter by another family. Her name was Marley. Immediately we felt this was the dog for our household even though she had kennel-cough and a few not-so-good habits. If no one else claimed her, it would be just a few weeks before her life would be ended to make room for another animal for adoption. While this seems harsh, there were only so many places available at the animal shelter. So, the first point in this story is—without redemption by adoption, she was destined for death.

After bringing Marley home, there was still a lot to be worked through. While we made a commitment to her, she still had to make a commitment to us by adapting to our household ways and eventually giving and receiving affection. This is our house and to live with us requires an assent to our ways; we would not be living according to her ways. (The previous family that brought her to their home returned her for incompatibility reasons.) The second point in this story is—joining our family and receiving the privileges afforded in our family required Marley to adapt to our ways.

On our part there was love and affection to be offered, good food, a doggy bed, warmth, reasonable exercise, and health care. All Marley had to do was be a dog, give and receive affection, not tear up our house, and tell us when she needed to go outside for natural functions. To instill these things in her required time and interaction. She has lived with us for ten years now, and our family has a wonderful relationship with Marley, but it took time to develop. The third point in this story is—there is a training period to successfully integrate into a household, even after some level of commitment has been made.

Applying Marley's Story to Your Life

As you read on, you will discover the three points we made in our story about Marley somehow mirror our condition in initiating a walk with God. The first point, similar to the story above, is that we naturally do not obey God's family ways of behavior: we are, unknowingly, under the sentence of death–not in an immediate natural way, but in a supernatural way. We all fall short of God's standards and need to be rescued.

> ... *the Lord Jesus will be ... dealing out retribution to those who do not know God and to those who do not obey the gospel of our Lord Jesus. These will pay the penalty of eternal destruction, away from the presence of the Lord and from the glory of His power ... [i.e., in hell].*
>
> *2 Thessalonians 1:7–9*

While most of our transgressions will not take us to immediate physical death, they do lead to a spiritual death—an eternal separation from God and His household—when our body eventually dies. In a way, similar to the rescue of our dog, Marley, from the animal shelter, God has made a way for you as a human being to join His family and escape death. His open invitation to us all, regardless of our deeds of transgression, is stated in the Bible:

> *For God so loved the world, that He gave His only begotten Son, that whoever believes in Him shall not perish, but have eternal life.*
>
> *John 3:16*

Salvation – Redemption

So, how can we respond to this invitation to join God's family through His Son, Jesus Christ? While not immediately obvious, it is quite simple—just like our story about Marley. As a human being there will be a few adjustments we will need to make in our thinking and actions in joining God's family (household); we'll get to those later. But first, there's a simple prayer on the next page that we can say to God in accepting His invitation.

Salvation -
Like Receiving
Our Heavenly Citizenship

When you have prayed this prayer with a sincere and believing heart, you become a Christian. The declaration you just made is similar to immigrating and becoming a citizen of another country. As a heavenly citizen (member of God's family), you will now have the privileges of His family (all of the promises of the Bible, including those highlighted in this book), of knowing God here on earth and joining Him in heaven when your earthly body dies. You have just passed through the gateway to eternal life. However, it is necessary to understand that your salvation (new earthly life in Christ), while it has a beginning point in time, is not completed until you have entered heaven.

148

Salvation Prayer

- Dear Heavenly Father, I come to You now in the name of Your only begotten Son, Jesus.

- I acknowledge that I have not known You nor lived my life according to Your righteous ways.

- Therefore, I have been headed on a course away from You towards hell.

- I ask that You forgive me for my sinful ways. I choose to change my ways and live my life according to Your ways.

- I gratefully accept the work Jesus did in suffering the penalty of my sins in His body and dying on the cross that I might live.

- I believe that You, Heavenly Father, raised Jesus from the dead.

- I ask that You receive me now as Your child, through the precious blood that Jesus shed for me.

- I ask that You reveal Yourself to me further, and that You would strengthen me to be able to walk in Your ways.   Amen.

While the initiation of your new life as a child of God is similar in concept to receiving a new passport, one that identifies you as a citizen of heaven, there is something more. Effectively, you also receive a ticket for your future journey to your new country, heaven, when your earthly body eventually dies.

Lordship

Now, having escaped eternal death and damnation through receiving Jesus, we need to turn our attention to the second point highlighted in our story about Marley. We, in a similar way, need to alter our old ways of living to begin to mirror God's ways and enter into compatibility with His family—there are some changes that need to be made. Accepting God's invitation to eternal life is the beginning, but not the end. Just as our new family member, Marley, needed to adapt to our ways, so we too will need to adjust to God's family. Of course, having worked your way through this book will be helpful to you as you will have at least twelve areas of conformance to God's family under your belt.

It would be good to tell God your deep wish to enter into His ways and ask Him for help since we as ordinary human beings, by ourselves, are not strong enough to deeply conform to His ways. In the story about our dog, we needed to make known our family ways to Marley and help her begin to conform: It was a process. And so, it will be with us in learning to conform to God's family ways. But since you can speak human language, you can ask questions, read the Bible, pray, etc. It should be a little easier for you. Just as we helped Marley adapt to our household, God Himself can and will enter into the process to assist you in adapting to His family.

Many of us have met those who claim to be of the household of God, saying they are Christians, but not manifesting the character of God, the love of God, nor the righteousness of God. Maybe they accepted the invitation of God to eternal life, but they never really decided to adapt to His ways. Perhaps the testimony of their lives has put you off from both God and church. Let's for a moment consider what their problem is so that we don't become like that. Perhaps a simple illustration will help.

> We can buy a horse to ride. When we've paid for it, the horse belongs to us. However, if it has never been ridden, there is a behavior modification process that the horse must pass through for it to be suitable for riding. Various techniques can be used to bring the horse into submission so that it may be ridden. But until the horse gives over its will, it is of no use to its master; it will not obey nor serve his purposes and pleasure.

Many Christians are like horses that cannot be ridden. Although they have been bought by the blood of Jesus and have acknowledged Him as God, they have never given the Lord full access to their lives.

Although we may have acknowledged Jesus as Lord in His position as Deity, we may never have submitted ourselves and all that we have and are to Him personally. If this is our condition, Jesus is, in fact, not our Lord. You are invited to change from that position to enter a deeper relationship with God, to more fully live your life for Jesus, by praying the "Lordship Prayer" of dedication and submission found on the next page.

Lordship Prayer

Lord Jesus, I acknowledge my need of You, and I accept You as my Savior, my Redeemer, my Lord, and my Deliverer.

I invite You to be Lord of my whole life:
- Over my spirit—my prayers, my worship, my spiritual understanding, my creativity, and my conscience
- Over my mind—my thoughts, my memories, my dreams
- Over my emotions—my feelings and emotional expressions and responses

- Over my will—all my decisions and purposing

    I invite You to be Lord over my body:
- Over my eyes—all that I look at and over every look that I give outward
- Over my ears and all that I listen to
- Over my nose and all that comes into it
- Over my mouth and all that goes into it and every word that comes out of it
- Over my sexuality
- Over all my physical activities

I invite You to be Lord over all my relationships: past, present, and future.
I invite You to be Lord over my resources: time, energy, finances, property, and all that I have.
I invite You to be Lord over the time and manner of my death.
Come, Lord Jesus, and take Your rightful place in all the areas of my life.
Thank You that Your blood was shed that I might be set free from the influence of selfishness and Satan.

Amen.

The Next Steps—
Perhaps You Were Wondering . . .

John Wimber, keyboard artist, vocalist, song writer and manager of the secular, popular and influential Righteous Brothers band in the early 1960's, miraculously received Jesus as his Savior one evening in the Nevada desert following one of their Las Vegas stage shows. He began to go to church with his wife, subsequently read through the Bible and attended Bible college. But he began to wonder, "When do we do the stuff, the stuff that Jesus did?" While those things weren't happening in the denomination whose church he attended, he went on to experience God in some ways similar to the things we've written about in this book. He planted a new, non-denominational church and engendered the planting of many others, founding a movement, the Association of Vineyard Churches, circling the globe that did, at that time, embrace such practices.

Perhaps you, having read and prayed through the chapters of this book, are wondering something like John Wimber wondered. As a foundation for this next step, let's revisit what we've learned, both in the chapters of the book and here in the appendix. Let's see how you can "Do the stuff that Jesus did!"

Entering God's Family Behavior

Marley's story could only take us so far in developing and understanding our relationship with God because, after all, she is only a dog and we are human beings. The points from her story that mirror entering Christian life are:

1. Our escape from death

2. Our coming into God's family, provisions, privileges, and family behavior
3. Our time of adaptation to His ways—in Christian terms—entering discipleship

The third point, the time for us to adapt to God's ways, is similar in concept, but for human beings, there is a great deal more available to us; for example, developing the ability to be able to enter into and participate in the works of God here on earth (the very things John Wimber was wondering about). In the rest of this *Appendix*, we are going to examine just what we need to walk through in the process of adopting God's ways to become a born-again believer and disciple of the Lord Jesus Christ.

Perhaps as you read some of the true, illustrative stories in this book, you wondered just how they happened and how we knew what to do to help someone in such dramatic and amazing ways to bring about God's kind purposes. Keep in mind that God is the one bringing about the miraculous work; we are only assisting. Beyond having compassionate, merciful hearts, we only need two main supernatural abilities to participate:

- First of all, we need to situationally be able to see (discern) what God wants to do.
- Secondly, in each of the miraculous works of God, we need to be able to act/enter (participate) in the process to facilitate what He is doing.

The Bible, in fact, does promise that we will be participating with God in some of His supernatural works:

*Truly, truly, I say to you, he who believes in Me, the
works that I do, he will do also; and greater works
than these he will do; because I go to the Father.*
John 14:12

When we first read this Scripture, most of us have trouble
believing it. But the apostle Paul's letter to the church at
Ephesus tells us that one of the purposes for which God
made us is to do the works of Jesus:

*For we are His workmanship, created in Christ Jesus
for good works, which God prepared beforehand so
that we would walk in them.*
Ephesians 2:10

In this final section of the *Appendix*, we are going to
examine the second and third steps of being born-again (the
first step being salvation): the two baptisms that help you
enter into the most exciting of lifelong adventures to be
able to do the same kind of things God has recorded in the
Bible and that we've testified to. Are you ready?

The Two Baptisms

There was a man named Nicodemus in ancient Jerusalem
who wondered just how Jesus was able to perform His
dramatic miracles throughout the nation. Coming to Him in
the evening, Nicodemus began to inquire how it was
possible. Jesus' answers involve two kinds of baptisms, one
of water and one of Spirit. Let's join Nicodemus and Jesus
in the dialogue, remembering the supernatural abilities
named in the previous section (discerning what God wants
to do and entering into His works). Nicodemus has just

inquired how these works are possible and Jesus' first cryptical response is:

> *Jesus answered and said to him, "Truly, truly, I say to you, unless one is born again, he cannot see the kingdom of God."*
>
> *John 3:3*

The conversation was originally spoken in either ancient Hebrew or Aramaic, but recorded for us, not in English, but in Greek. In the English language, the word *see* in this verse is translated from the Greek word ὁράω (horaō), which means "to see, recognize, perceive, or attend to." Now this is getting just a little exciting: Jesus has just mentioned that the first ability we need to participate in the works of God (as noted in the previous section)— is situationally being able to see (discern) what God wants to do. But now we wonder, "Just what does it mean to be "born again"? Nicodemus is also puzzled by Jesus' response and asks Him to clarify this response.

> *Jesus answered, "Truly, truly, I say to you, unless one is born of water and the Spirit he cannot enter into the kingdom of God."*
>
> *John 3:5*

In answering Nicodemus' inquiry into how He could perform such miracles as He did throughout the nation, Jesus is now showing us how we can participate, act/enter in(to) the supernatural kingdom works in which God wants you to participate/facilitate here on earth in your lifetime. In the preceding section, this is the second ability we are seeking to join God in doing His works. Now we are in a better position than Nicodemus was, needing only to understand the two baptisms (one of water and one of Spirit). Let's now look further into these two baptisms. (Fortunately, there are plenty of biblical texts to help us.) Let's go on.

Water Baptism

Following our belief in Jesus and giving our whole life to Him, water baptism is the next part of being "born-again" (see John 3:1–21). In His conversation with Nicodemus, Jesus reveals two important pieces of information about seeing (what God is doing supernaturally) and entering (stepping into) His Kingdom works. We must experience the process of being born into His Kingdom through both the medium of (a) water and (b) Spirit.

Since God is Spirit, if we are going to encounter Him and do His works (i.e., carry out our life assignment from God), we must be able to meet/discern Him in the spiritual realm. We need to see, hear, and operate both in the natural earthly realm and in the spiritual realm where He dwells (the Kingdom of God). To enter His Kingdom works, we must be "born again." Please bear with us; while this is simple, many churches do not carefully bring this to the attention of their congregations.

Entering the Kingdom—
The Next Key: Being Born of Water

Unless we are born again (into His Kingdom), we cannot really know God because we cannot hear, see, or perceive what He is doing. Further, if we can't sense what He is doing, we cannot enter into God's works as Jesus did.

A wonderful, but sometimes confusing, tension exists in Scripture concerning the "Kingdom of God." Sometimes this phrase refers to the coming heavenly age, both that which is in heaven and that which will be manifest when Jesus returns to the earth. But there is even a third concept—the Kingdom being seen, being understood, and breaking through into this present evil age, thereby being made manifest by those who have entered into the "Kingdom of God" by becoming born-again. Those who are born-again (initiated into His Kingdom) will do the works of Jesus. Be careful here, as some churches say that merely believing in Jesus makes you "born-again"; this is not the complete truth, only part of it.

In the previous section we saw that making Jesus Lord of every area of our life means we must die (step away from) to our personal desires where they clash with those of Jesus. This is because they are not founded on furthering the wishes of God the Father. In the "Lordship Prayer" we gave Jesus lordship of every area of our life. Now we will link this dying to self with water baptism.

In Scripture we find two progressive revelations in regard to water baptism. The first is the baptism of repentance introduced and performed by John the Baptist.

> *... and they were being baptized by him in the Jordan River, as they confessed their sins.*
>
> *Matthew 3:6*

This baptism for repentance from sin was both a public confession of sin and an outward declaration of an inward change in attitude away from sin. As Jesus' ministry increased, John the Baptist's decreased, but Jesus' disciples continued what John initiated.

The second revelation regarding water baptism begins in the last chapter of Matthew. After Jesus' resurrection, He commands His disciples to baptize each new believer or convert (a beginning disciple) into the three Persons of God:

> *Go therefore and make disciples of all the nations, baptizing them in the name of the Father and the Son and the Holy Spirit ...*
>
> *Matthew 28:19*

Again, this baptism commanded by Jesus incorporates confession and repentance for sin. But something more is added to what John the Baptist and Jesus' disciples are doing at the beginning of the Gospels. Jesus introduced a new element here: being baptized into the Father and the Son and the Holy Spirit—the complete godhead. The Bible explains:

As we go under the waters of baptism, we are making a break with our former worldly and self-oriented lives. We are being baptized into Jesus' death as we die to ourselves. Going under the water symbolizes death. As we arise from the water, we are being raised into the family of God the Father and into the life of Jesus (Romans 6:4–5; Colossians 2:12b).

It is important to understand that Jesus commanded the sacrament of water baptism. It is more than a symbolic exercise; something spiritual happens to us when we obey His directive. To some, the results are dramatically noticeable and to others they are not immediately, experientially obvious. But something always occurs in and for us in the spiritual realm. Baptism is an act of faith.

A Closer Look at the Process of Baptism

Having been born of water, we are now nearly ready to look at the second key to the Kingdom of God: being born of Spirit. Before we progress further, though, we need to examine more closely the underlying Greek word that is translated (transliterated) into our word *baptize*. This word, associated with both of the keys to the Kingdom of God (by water and Spirit), is the Greek word βαπτίζω, *baptizō*: to dip, sink.

Conceptually, this word means "to totally immerse and saturate in." It also means "a ceremonial washing or cleansing in which all of the body is dipped or immersed." It does not mean to be sprinkled or poured upon, nor does it mean to be touched or dampened by a wet object. If we were to baptize a ship, for example, we would need to push it under the surface of the water. When the ship was finally covered by the waters, then we could say it had been baptized.

Baptism is a physical act that has spiritual consequences. We are not saying baptism must drown us, only that we go under the water for a moment. We must be obedient to the commands of the Lord. All that is within us of our fleshly (soul-controlled) life is to be spiritually put to death, to rise again in Christ Jesus to the purposes and plans of God.

Entering the Kingdom—
The Last Key: Being Born of the Spirit
(Being Baptized in the Holy Spirit)

Let's revisit the discussion with Nicodemus from John 3. Here Jesus tells him, in outline form, how to enter the Kingdom of God. The context of this Scripture is Nicodemus' inquiry into how Jesus was able to perform Kingdom (of God) works.

Jesus' answer draws Nicodemus from his natural, worldly thinking into a deeper mystery. But Jesus reveals the mystery to us:

> *Jesus answered and said to him, "Truly, truly, I say to you, unless one is born again, he cannot see the kingdom of God."*
>
> *John 3:3*

Jesus is answering Nicodemus in light of John 5:19, explaining that He (Himself, who has been born of both water and Spirit) is only doing what He sees the Father doing. Let's remind ourselves how Jesus later explains a healing miracle to a group of Jews:

> *Therefore, Jesus answered and was saying to them, "Truly, truly, I say to you, the Son can do nothing of Himself, unless it is something He sees the Father doing; for whatever the Father does, these things the Son also does in like manner."*
>
> *John 5:19*

Nicodemus did not understand Jesus' answer, sounding more puzzled in his next question. So, Jesus gives him (and us) the keys we began discussing in the last section:

> *Jesus answered, "Truly, truly, I say to you, unless one is born of water and the Spirit he cannot enter into the kingdom of God."*
>
> *John 3:5*

The explanation of the mystery is as follows: To do the works of God requires that we be born again. Part of that process is being baptized into Christ, His death and resurrection, in the baptism sacrament known as baptism in water. But the first baptism (in water) needs to be followed by a baptism of another kind. This second medium is the Holy Spirit. How does this baptism occur? While we can pray for someone and even lay hands on them to be baptized in the Holy Spirit, ultimately it is Jesus who must manifest His presence and clothe them in the power of the Holy Spirit as on the day of Pentecost (Acts 2). Let's look at what Jesus has to say about being baptized in the Holy Spirit:

> *... for John baptized with water, but you will be baptized with the Holy Spirit not many days from now.*
>
> *Acts 1:5*

> *And behold, I am sending forth the promise of My Father upon you; but you are to stay in the city until you are clothed with power from on high.*
>
> *Luke 24:49*

Nicodemus is puzzled over how Jesus was able to do His amazing works, but we now have understanding. Those who do the works of Jesus today are empowered to do them through baptism in the Holy Spirit. This knowledge helps us with another mystery: How are we personally going to be able to fulfill Jesus' expectation for us? James helps us understand that the works of "born-again" believers are the hallmark of their faith and salvation:

> *What use is it, my brethren, if someone says he has faith but he has no works? Can that faith save him?*
> *James 2:14*

> *For just as the body without the spirit is dead, so also faith without works is dead.*
> *James 2:26*

So, we begin to understand that a "born-again" (of water and the Spirit) disciple (Christian) will manifest the works of Jesus in his or her life. Those who are moving into increased intimacy with God can expect to see the works of the Father and, by means of the Holy Spirit, join Him in what He is doing. These works are the supernatural outcome of knowing God as our Father through Jesus Christ.

Now that we know *why* we need to be baptized in the Spirit, let's take a look at *how* we are born of the Spirit. Earlier we read in Luke that Jesus will send forth the promised baptism in the Spirit:

*And behold, I am sending forth the promise of My
Father upon you; but you are to stay in the city until
you are clothed with power from on high.*

Luke 24:49

This promise was first voiced by John the Baptist, who
heralded Jesus as the Messiah:

*I baptized you with water; but He will baptize you with
the Holy Spirit.*

Mark 1:8

Jesus is the one who baptizes us in the Holy Spirit.
Therefore, in seeking this baptism, we need to ask Jesus to
come and flood, bathe, and overwhelm us with the presence
of His Holy Spirit.

As at Pentecost (Acts 2) and at Cornelius' house (Acts 10),
we may be overwhelmed, clothed in power, and flooded
with the presence of the Holy Spirit without anyone visibly
or discernibly touching us. However, Jesus may also use a
person to pray over and lay hands on us. This experience
can somehow impart the presence of the Spirit and initiate a
Spirit baptism experience:

*[Peter and John came down] and prayed for them that
they might receive the Holy Spirit. For He had not yet
fallen upon any of them; they had simply been [water]
baptized in the name of the Lord Jesus. Then they
began laying their hands on them, and they were
receiving the Holy Spirit.*

Acts 8:15–17

Two practical questions about baptism in the Spirit need to be addressed:

1. How will I know if I have been baptized in the Holy Spirit?
2. What would keep me from being baptized in the Holy Spirit?

Let's take a look at some answers.

Sensations of Holy Spirit Baptism

Baptism in the Holy Spirit is often both a spiritual and natural (i.e., physical) experience. Therefore, when it happens to us, most will know we have been baptized in the Holy Spirit. However, the effects and sensations will vary from one person to the next.

- You may be filled with joy and laughter, feel the power of God upon you (which could cause you to temporarily physically collapse or fall to the ground), become very weak, feel heat or tingling sensations, see visions, hear the voice of God, speak in tongues (a language not known to you). Following baptism in the Holy Spirit, God's spiritual gifts (for which you need this empowering) will begin to manifest in your life.
- If you haven't experienced something physically/ spiritually and have not received any of the Spirit's supernatural gifts, then you probably have not yet been baptized in the Holy Spirit. Keep seeking and asking God about any blockages that you have to receive Him in this necessary step and continue to ask those who have already been baptized in the

Holy Spirit to lay hands on you and pray for this baptism.

Blockages to Holy Spirit Baptism*

A number of factors may delay your being baptized in the Holy Spirit. The first consideration is whether you are actively seeking God for this blessing. He comes to those who are seeking Him with all their heart (Jeremiah 29:13).

Another factor that hinders receiving Holy Spirit baptism is permission. Have you given God permission to do anything that He wants with you, at any time and in any situation? Trusting Him is necessary. Of course, you need to have received Jesus as your Savior and made Jesus the Lord of your life. (Normally you would have been baptized in water first, but sometimes God does things in the opposite order.)

Certain spiritual blockages can also prevent our being baptized in the Holy Spirit.

- Unrenounced claims of false religions—personal and generational practices, including oaths, dedication rituals, and invitations to false gods who inhabit or act in and through you.
- Participation in martial arts or Freemasonry, the Communist Party and youth groups, and other organized spiritual activities or groups, including Satanism and witchcraft.
- Involvement in astrology, soul travel, and/or heavy metal (hard rock and other occult-based) music.
- If you belong or have belonged to a denomination or church that believes or teaches against baptism in

the Spirit, you may need to forgive them for this
doctrine and renounce this belief for yourself.

*Unconfessed sin—personal and generational occult practices, such
as hypnotism, astrology, water witching, séances to speak or
commune with the dead, spiritism, and/or babka (or witch doctor)
healing.

Other books by Otto Bixler

Widows, Orphans, and Prisoners

A "How to" book written to bring spiritual freedom to those with a family inheritance of, or personal experience under, Russian communism. But there is amazing life application for those from western nations. There are no boundaries on God's truth and love.

No matter what country you're from:

- Find out what God thinks is important
- Discover how to remove key spiritual blockages from your life
- Experience new holiness and spiritual power to do the works of Jesus
- Begin to hear God like never before

It Isn't Free and It Isn't Masonry

Discover the surprising source of many of life's problems. Some of them are rooted in Freemasonry in your direct family bloodline or by personal involvement. These result in personal problems not usually attributed to this source. This book will help you discover, diagnose and remove them.

Join the many who can now live their lives as God intended. Mental freedom, spiritual sensitivity and freedom, physical restoration from many maladies, recovery from financial difficulties – all are attainable to those seeking help from God to set them free from the curses of Freemasonry.

Ingram Content Group UK Ltd.
Milton Keynes UK
UKHW021837160623
423552UK00013B/363

9 798885 254175